Hoosier Cabinets

Philip D. Kennedy

Published by
Philip D. Kennedy
9256 Holyoke Court
Indianapolis, IN 46268

First Edition
Ninth Printing - 1999

International Standard Book Number: 0-9622831-1-8
Library of Congress Catalog Number: 89-91293

Printed in the United States of America

Contents

Acknowledgements

The author is sincerely grateful to those who gave of their time and shared their knowledge to make this book possible. I would especially like to thank the Henry County Historical Society for allowing me to research their extensive files on the Hoosier Manufacturing Company. I would also like to thank Ray Striker of South Bend, Indiana for so much of the information about G.I. Sellers & Sons. Formerly of Elwood, Indiana. Mr. Striker is the grandson of G.I. Sellers.

I would also like to thank the following individuals and organizations for their help:

Dale Allgood, D & D Antiques, Indianapolis, Indiana
Clinton County Historical Society, Frankfort, Indiana
Coppes Napanee, Nappanee, Indiana
Elwood Public Library, Elwood, Indiana
Frankfort Public Library, Frankfort, Indiana
Sandy Grove, ETC., Brownsburg, Indiana
Ned Griner, Muncie, Indiana
Hartman's Furniture, Nappanee, Indiana
Indiana State Library, Indianapolis, Indiana
Lebanon Public Library, Lebanon, Indiana
Tom Loser, Ellettsville, Indiana
Nappanee Public Library, Nappanee, Indiana
New Castle Public Library, New Castle, Indiana
Bernard J. Schuck, Elwood, Indiana
Charles Short, Elwood, Indiana
Ken Wayman, Mooresville, Indiana

I would like to thank my mother, Evelyn Kennedy, for proofreading much of the text. Her enthusiasm for the book has made the project even more worthwhile. Finally, I would like to thank my wife, Phyllis, for her support and encouragement. This book was her idea and it is based primarily on her collection of old advertisements for kitchen cabinets.

Preface

A few years ago, when my wife was starting her antique furniture business, we bought an oak step-back kitchen cabinet at an auction. A friend who was attending the auction with us remarked that we had just bought a nice "Hoosier" cabinet. After making a few repairs, we advertised our "Hoosier" in a local paper. When a caller asked if our cabinet was made by The Hoosier Manufacturing Company, I told him that I thought "Hoosier" was a generic term used to describe old kitchen cabinets such as ours. The gentleman informed me that there had indeed been a Hoosier Manufacturing Company which had built many kitchen cabinets. Although The Hoosier Manufacturing Company was one of the largest producers of kitchen cabinets, other companies such as Sellers, Napanee, Boone, and McDougall made large numbers of cabinets. Since all of these companies were located in Indiana, the Hoosier state, the term "Hoosier" cabinet has become universal when referring to these old kitchen cabinets.

A few weeks later, we purchased our first real Hoosier cabinet. The cabinet was in very good condition and it had everything including the flour bin, sugar bin, spice jar rack and even the cardboard inserts inside the upper doors. The only thing wrong with our Hoosier was that the roll doors were coming apart and some of the slats were badly warped. Replacement doors were not readily available then and we spent a lot of time straightening the slats and rebuilding the roll doors. When we finished, the cabinet was nearly perfect and we sold it very quickly– too quickly. I still wish we had that cabinet as we have never found another Hoosier that had all the original parts and was in such good condition.

After that first Hoosier, we bought several more. Most of them had several coats of stubborn paint and were often missing essential parts. In the next few years, we completely rebuilt several Hoosier cabinets. We also restored Sellers, Napanee, Boone, McDougall and other old kitchen cabinets. Three of the Hoosier cabinets we later bought were in such bad condition that we bought them just for the parts. However, we could not bring ourselves to destroy these once fine old cabinets and so we eventually rebuilt them also.

We are no longer in the antique furniture business. We were having difficulty finding hardware and parts for the Hoosier cabinets and other furniture that we restored. When we found sources for those items, we began to stock them for ourselves and other furniture restorers. Today, we have a thriving restoration hardware business. Since we specialize in parts and hardware for Hoosier and other kitchen cabinets, we have assembled a collection of old advertisements and other information pertaining to "Hoosier" cabinets. Customers often request "all the information we have on Hoosier cabinets." Since that information would fill a book, we have only been able to answer specific questions regarding Hoosiers and other kitchen cabinets. Many of our customers and friends have suggested the we write a book on Hoosier cabinets. *Hoosier Cabinets* is the result of those requests.

This book is written for anyone who owns a "Hoosier" cabinet, is looking for one, or is planning to restore one. Although this book is primarily about The Hoosier Manufacturing Company and its line of Hoosier kitchen cabinets, we have included information about Boone, McDougall, Napanee, Sellers, and other kitchen cabinets. Where possible, we have given short histories about the companies that made these other cabinets. This book contains many old advertisements for kitchen cabinets, some dating back to 1905. These advertisements have proved invaluable to us when attempting to identify or date old cabinets. This book also includes many photographs of old kitchen cabinets. Most of these photographs include descriptive captions identifying the maker and features of the particular cabinet. The final section of the book is about the restoration of old kitchen cabinets and includes many of the techniques we have learned while restoring Hoosier and other cabinets. We hope that you will enjoy this book and profit from it.

Philip D. Kennedy

1

Introduction to "Hoosier" Cabinets

The origin of the "Hoosier" cabinet can be traced back to the baker's cabinets of the late 1800s. The typical baker's cabinet consisted of a kitchen table with drawers and two large bins for flour or meal. It also included a upper section with shelves for storing dishes and other utensils. This upper shelf section often included two doors with glass panels. As the baker's cabinet evolved into the "Hoosier" cabinet, the lower section was replaced with a cabinet base that had a door on one side for storing cooking utensils and drawers on the other side. The upper section was divided into storage areas with wood or glass doors and some early cabinets had a row of small drawers below the doors. Later refinements included built-in flour sifters, sugar containers, and spice jars. The wood table tops of the very early cabinets were often covered with zinc sheet metal. When the zinc was found to be toxic, it was replaced with aluminum. Later the metal-covered work tops were replaced by porcelain tops that pulled out for added work space,

By the turn of the century several small furniture factories in the Midwest began making kitchen cabinets. Eventually, a few of these factories had grown into large manufacturing companies producing many thousands of cabinets a year. The largest of these companies, The Hoosier Manufacturing Company, had produced two million cabinets by 1920. The "Hoosier" cabinet continued to be popular through the 1920s. However, by the early 1930s the demand for these cabinets fell as built-in kitchen cabinets began to appear. By 1940 only a few "Hoosier" cabinets were being built.

In order to better understand the role of the "Hoosier" cabinet, it might be helpful to reflect on life in a typical Midwestern town in the early 1920s. There were no radios then and the only communications most people had with the outside world were newspapers and magazines. Few people owned automobiles and people traveled to work or downtown on street cars. Smaller towns often had no means of public transportation and people walked or rode bicycles to their destinations.

The average home was certainly sparse by today's standards. Although most homes had electricity and running water, the only means of refrigeration was the ice box where perishables were kept chilled by large blocks of ice. Since food did not keep long in these old ice boxes, daily trips to the grocery store were often necessary. Cooking stoves were fueled by gas, kerosene, or even wood. The typical housewife spent a great deal of her time in the kitchen baking bread, cakes, and pies and preparing meals. The "Hoosier" cabinet represents an era most of us never knew. Yet these cabinets were so much a part of the daily lives of our mothers or grandmothers. It is certainly a part of Americana worth preserving.

What is a Hoosier Cabinet?

In recent years the term "Hoosier" cabinet has been used rather loosely to refer to free-standing kitchen cabinets made from the turn of the century to the mid 1930s. These cabinets usually have porcelain work tops, roll doors, and built-in flour sifters that held 50 pounds or more of flour. Many of these cabinets were also equipped with tin bread drawers, sugar jars, spice jars, pull-out bread boards, and countless other features designed to provide the housewife with a "modern, efficient kitchen." Many of these cabinets and their features were advertised in popular magazines of the day including *The Saturday Evening Post, Better Homes and Gardens*, and *The Ladies Home Journal*.

In addition to providing about 40 inches of counter space, these cabinets stored cooking utensils, dishes, and most staple items found in kitchens of that era. Many of the early magazine ads reproduced in this book show opened cabinets filled with an amazing array of items. It is hard to imagine how our mothers or grandmothers managed their kitchens with so little cabinet space when compared to today's modern kitchens where counter space and cabinet space are often measured in tens of feet rather than inches.

The name Hoosier Cabinet can be attributed to The Hoosier Manufacturing Company of New Castle, Indiana. Founded in 1898, Hoosier had built more than two million cabinets by 1920. Our research indicates that The Hoosier Manufacturing Company was the most prolific builder of early kitchen cabinets. By 1921 there were approximately 20 million households in the United States. Since two million, or ten percent, of the homes in America had kitchen cabinets built by The Hoosier Manufacturing Company, it is quite easy to see how the name "Hoosier" cabinet became so popular.

Other large manufacturers of early kitchen cabinets were: Sellers, Napanee, Boone, McDougall. All of these cabinets were built in Indiana, the Hoosier state. There were many smaller manufacturers of kitchen cabinets located in Indiana and throughout the Midwest. Since most of these smaller companies had limited marketing resources and did little or no national advertising, there is hardly any information available about their cabinets.

Oak kitchen cabinet dating back to the late 1890s or early 1900s. This style of cabinet is often called a baker's cabinet or "possum belly" cabinet. The two large bins in the bottom section are for flour or meal. Note the row of small drawers under the doors. Manufacturer is unknown.

If you have a cabinet made by one of the major manufacturers listed above, the magazine ads and photographs in this book should help in identifying and dating your cabinet. If you are in the process of restoring one of these cabinets, this information may help you to identify missing parts or hardware. If your cabinet is an "unknown" made by one of the smaller manufacturers, it may be difficult if not impossible to determine its origin. However, this should not make your cabinet less valuable or less desirable. Many of the cabinets built by these smaller companies are fine examples of the craftsmanship of an earlier time.

While most kitchen cabinet manufacturers flourished through the 1920s, many did not survive the great depression. Those companies that did survive the depression found themselves competing in a market where built-in kitchen cabinets were becoming commonplace. Most of these companies were out of business by the late 1930s, although the Sellers Company managed to survive until 1950 and Kitchen Maid lasted until 1965. Only one of the major manufacturers of early kitchen cabinets, Coppes Brothers of Nappanee, Indiana, which produced the popular Napanee cabinet, is still in business today. This company, although no longer owned by the Coppes family, now manufacturers modern built-in kitchen cabinets

Where to Find a Hoosier Cabinet

Since we sell restoration hardware for kitchen cabinets, many people call or write to ask where they can find an old kitchen cabinet such as a Hoosier or a Sellers. The answer to that question depends on such things as what part of the country you live in and whether you are looking for a cabinet to restore or a fully restored cabinet.

If you happen to live in the Midwest, you have a much better chance of finding a cabinet since most of them were made in this area of the country. If you are looking for a restored cabinet, I would advise shopping the antique dealers in your area until you find the cabinet you want. Although individuals sometimes advertise old kitchen cabinets in local newspapers and other advertising media, buying a cabinet in this manner can often prove time consuming and frustrating. You may drive several miles to see a cabinet that has been described by its owner as just what you have been looking for. When you finally arrive at the seller's home full of anticipation, you may be quite disappointed by a cabinet that bears no resemblance to the owner's description. However, this is not always the case. When we were in the antique furniture business, we made quite a few good buys from individuals.

Another source of cabinets is antique auctions. We have bought several cabinets from auction houses that specialize in antiques. In recent years antique auctions have been well

Oak kitchen cabinet. Circa 1900. This large cabinet has a zinc work top, glass paneled doors, and several drawers. The deep drawer on the right side was a flour bin that held a full sack of flour. The flour bin was fitted with casters so that it could be pulled out easily with its heavy load. This cabinet is similar to cabinets made by Hoosier, McDougall, Napanee, and other kitchen cabinet manufacturers at the turn of the century. The manufacturer of this cabinet is unknown.

advertised and are patronized by dealers, collectors and almost anyone else looking for antique furniture. It is not uncommon to find one or two "Hoosier" cabinets at a large antique auction, especially in the Midwest. Unless you are familiar with antique auctions, it is probably a good idea to attend a couple of auctions before buying a cabinet. This will give you an opportunity to become familiar with the auction procedures and avoid possible misunderstandings in the bidding process. Above all, inspect any pieces that may be of interest to you before the bidding begins. It is very easy to get caught up in the excitement of the bidding and then discover that you paid more than you intended for an item or that you bought something that you really didn't want.

If you are looking for a cabinet to restore, your search may be a little more difficult. At one time estate auctions were a good source of "furniture in the rough," a term used in the antique trade to describe furniture in need of restoration. However, the popularity of these auctions sometimes results in unrealistically high prices. But if you attend enough auctions, sooner or later you will find what you are looking for at a reasonable price. You may even be lucky enough to find a real bargain.

There are dealers who specialize in "furniture in the rough." These dealers, often referred to as "pickers" in the trade, spend much of their time searching for antique furniture. They in turn sell it to other dealers who restore furniture to sell in the retail market. Since many pickers sell only to other dealers, they are often difficult to find. Another source for cabinets in need of restoration are the large flea markets. These flea markets are usually open only one weekend each month. Most of the large regional flea markets advertise in local newspapers and antique trade journals. The antique trade journals, such as the *Antique Week* in the Midwest, also advertise most antique auctions in their regions. These advertisements often include complete listings of the items being offered for auction.

When you decide what type of cabinet you want, I would recommend that you visit several antique dealers, antique malls, and antique shows in your area. This will give you a good idea of what is available and what price you can expect to pay. Don't be in a hurry to buy your cabinet. Take the time to research the cabinets you are interested in so that you will know as much as possible about a cabinet before you buy it. If you are looking for a cabinet made by a major manufacturer such as Hoosier or Sellers, the old advertisements and photographs in this book should prove very helpful. Most of the advertisements show many details and features of a particular cabinet.

If you are buying a cabinet to restore, there are several things to consider. If the hardware is missing or broken, it will be difficult to find exact replacement latches unless the cabinet was made by The Hoosier Manufacturing Company. A wide variety of hardware and parts are available for the Hoosier, except for the flour sifter. The unique Hoosier flour sifter is almost impossible to find and it is unlikely that replacements will be made. Several styles

This Hoosier Special was purchased in 1925 by Mr. and Mrs. M.B. Weaver of Elkhart, Indiana. When the Weavers bought a new home in the mid-1930s, the Hoosier was moved to an enclosed porch. It was used until 1978 when Mrs. Weaver moved into a retirement home. Mrs. Weaver died in June of 1987 at the age of 101. This cabinet brings back many fond childhood memories. Mrs. Weaver was my grandmother. The cabinet is now part of our collection and is on display in our hardware showroom.

of hinges are available, but you may not be able to find the exact replacement hinge for a particular cabinet. For some cabinets, it may be necessary to replace all of the hardware with something other than the original. However, if the proper replacement hardware is selected, this may not be much of a problem. Hardware replacement is covered in greater detail in the *Restoring Hoosier Cabinets* section of this book.

Most "Hoosier" cabinets with porcelain work tops had metal side brackets which fastened the upper section to the cabinet base and allowed the porcelain top to be moved in and out. When the old cabinets were stored in basements or barns, the side brackets were often lost, misplaced, or even discarded. Until recently, replacement side brackets were almost impossible to find. When we were restoring "Hoosier" cabinets for resale, we passed up several nice cabinets at bargain prices because the side brackets were missing. Several styles of replacement side brackets are now available. If you have a cabinet with missing side brackets, you should be able to find replacements at reasonable prices.

Pricing a "Hoosier" Cabinet

We often receive phone calls or letters from people who want us to price their "Hoosier" cabinet. Of course, that would be impossible because there are so many variables that will determine the price for a particular cabinet. Prices tend to fluctuate considerably from one area to another. Prices for "Hoosier" cabinets are generally lower in the Midwest while they are quite high on the west coast. Prices even vary widely between dealers in the same area. For example, we found two Hoosier cabinets recently at a large antique show and the better cabinet of the two was priced about one-half the price of the other cabinet.

Another important factor in determining the price of a cabinet is its condition. A cabinet with original finish and in very good condition would be rare and would demand a very high price. Generally, "Hoosier" cabinets are found in every condition ranging from rough to completely restored. "Hoosier" cabinets that have been stored for years in leaky barns or sheds are likely to have considerable water damage. Since such a cabinet would require a great deal of work to restore, it would be worth very little. However, a cabinet that is complete and has been carefully stored in a dry basement or similar storage area may bring a rather high price.

There are also many factors that determine the value of a "restored" cabinet. The ideal restoration is a cabinet that has been restored as close to original condition as possible with careful attention to detail. Due to the cost and time involved, such an approach is not practical for most antique furniture dealers. Since "Hoosier" cabinets are rather complex and most have seen many years of hard use or neglect, they are usually one of the most difficult pieces of furniture to restore. You can expect to find restored "Hoosier" cabinets ranging from very poor to excellent and you should expect them to be priced accordingly.

Occasionally you will find a "Hoosier" cabinet that has been put together using parts of two or more different cabinets. In the antique trade such a cabinet is referred to as a *married* piece. Most often a married "Hoosier" cabinet consists of the base unit of one cabinet and the top section of another cabinet. Careful inspection can usually detect a married cabinet. This is especially true when the married piece consists of two well known cabinets such as a Hoosier and a Sellers. A skilled restorer may be able to create a married cabinet that would not be detected by most people. Although a married cabinet may be quite suitable for the needs of some people, it should be noted that such a piece is less valuable than an original cabinet.

Cabinets made of oak almost always command higher prices than cabinets made from other woods such as poplar, gumwood, or maple. A missing flour sifter can reduce the price of a cabinet $100 or more. Other missing components and accessories will similarly affect the price of a cabinet. A cabinet with original hardware in good condition will bring a premium price. If some of the hardware has been replaced, it should match the original as closely as possible.

Because there are so many things that can determine the value of a particular cabinet, we have made no attempt to include a price guide in this book. However, the information contained in this book should prove helpful in determining the condition of a particular cabinet and, therefore, its relative value.

This is an example of a married cabinet. The upper section is from a Sellers cabinet and the lower section is a Hoosier. Since the upper section is somewhat narrower than the base, a wood spacer was used to mount the side brackets on each side of the cabinet.

2

The Hoosier Manufacturing Company and the Hoosier Cabinet

The Hoosier Manufacturing Company was founded in 1898 in Albany, Indiana, a small town about 65 miles northeast of Indianapolis. The company was established when an Albany banker James S. McQuinn, his son Emmett G. McQuinn, and two partners, J.M. Maring and T.F. Hart, gained control of a defunct Albany furniture factory. J.M. Maring became president of the new organization, T.F. Hart was vice president, and James S. McQuinn was secretary-treasurer and general manager. Emmett G. McQuinn, although a rather young man at the time, was appointed office manager of the new company.

Much of the history of The Hoosier Manufacturing Company operations at Albany has been lost. Although we are not sure what other products may have been manufactured at the Albany factory, we are fairly certain that kitchen cabinets were produced there. Soon after The Hoosier Manufacturing Company was established, the Albany factory was destroyed by a fire. Although many historical accounts date the time of the fire as January of 1899, our research indicates that the factory burned in January of 1900. Within a few days after the fire, the owners decided to relocate their fledging enterprise to New Castle, a growing industrial town about 25 miles south of Albany.

After looking at two possible sites, they decided to acquire the factory of the former Speeder Cycle Company, a bicycle manufacturer. The Speeder Cycle factory was located on the south edge of town in an area that was mostly farm land at that time. Even though the site was only a little over a mile from the center of town, it was considered a long way from town then. It must be remembered that the automobile was still a novelty in 1900 and most workers depended on walking or bicycles for transportation. However, the Speeder factory was relatively new with 18,000 feet of floor space, and there was plenty of ground available for expansion. The town of New Castle agreed to pay $2,000 of the purchase price for the factory and the company signed a contract to employ 25 men for at least eight months a year.

The early Hoosier cabinets were built by skilled cabinetmakers and each cabinet was built from the ground up by a single cabinetmaker. The cabinet frames were partially built by workers in the woodworking shop and then sent to the assembly floor where the finished cabinets were completed. Each cabinetmaker spent a good deal of time fitting the doors, drawers and other parts that made the Hoosier cabinet. In those days a good cabinetmaker could produce about two cabinets a day, and the total output of the factory was about 10 cabinets a day.

All of this changed in 1903 when the company hired Harry A. Hall as general manager of the manufacturing operation. At that time the company employed about fifty people and the cabinets were still each built by individual cabinetmakers. One of the first changes instituted by Harry Hall was to standardize the line of cabinets built by the Hoosier company. The company built several sizes of cabinets and the parts were not interchangeable. Mr. Hall redesigned the line of Hoosier cabinets so that the sizes were standard and parts such as doors and drawers were interchangeable. For example, the same door could be used on several different styles of cabinets.

Next, Harry Hall changed the method by which the cabinets were manufactured when he introduced the assembly line to The Hoosier Manufacturing Company. Instead of each cabinet being built from the ground up by a single cabinetmaker, the parts were accurately machined and then the cabinets were progressively assembled with each workman performing a single operation. The results of these changes were uniform high quality cabinets and significantly increased production. In addition to his talents as a production manager, Harry Hall was also an inventor. He took out several patents related to the design and manufacture of Hoosier cabinets. These patents included a method of installing wood frames to make the porcelain tops rigid, a safety guard for saws, an improved sifter for the flour bins, and many others which are included in the collection of the Henry County Historical Society at New Castle.

Writing in the January, 1920 issue of the *Hoosier Bulletin*, James McQuinn, then president of The Hoosier Manufacturing Company, stated: "Mr. Hall has supervised personally the manufacture of nearly two million Hoosier cabinets, which is quite a number more than any other man in the United States has ever had anything to do with." The contribution Harry Hall made to the success of The Hoosier Manufacturing Company cannot be understated. Mr. Hall remained with the company until 1936.

By the end of 1903 The Hoosier Manufacturing Company was producing more cabinets than it was selling. At that time the Hoosier cabinets were sold by furniture dealers, many of whom were less than enthusiastic about selling kitchen cabinets. Almost from the beginning The Hoosier Manufacturing Company advertised nationally in leading magazines. They were receiving a large number of inquiries from their ads, but in many areas of the country there were no dealers to respond to these inquires. Many of those

This is the Hoosier Manufacturing Company complex about 1920. The main manufacturing building in the right background, the four story warehouse on the left, and the office building on the far left still remain. These buildings were used by a corrugated box company until the spring of 1988.

This is a portion of the main manufacturing building as it looks today. The original Speeder Cycle factory can be seen on the left. The smokestack shown here is the smaller smokestack in the picture above.

early magazine ads are reproduced in this book. After reading a few of these ads it is easy to see why the company received so much response from them.

When we began collecting Hoosier magazine ads several years ago we noticed that almost everyone of them gave a different address for The Hoosier Manufacturing Company. We wondered why such a large company would move so often. When we made our first trip to New Castle to do research for this book, we made a list of the various addresses and tried to find all of the locations where the company had operated. We soon discovered that The Hoosier Manufacturing Company had been located on South 14th Street since moving to New Castle in 1900. Later we learned that the addresses given in the various publications were fictitious. They were used to enable the company to know the source of each inquiry.

James McQuinn and his son, Emmett, began to work on a plan to sell more Hoosier cabinets. Emmett McQuinn was the first salesman to go out and call on dealers. In most instances he met almost total indifference to the Hoosier line and in some cases the dealers were even abusive. Early in 1904 the company announced a plan to sell Hoosier cabinets directly from the factory to the customer and eliminate the current dealers. They also began an extensive national advertising campaign to promote the Hoosier cabinets. Although we do not know all of the details, this plan called for the eventual establishment of a complete new dealer organization. A 1906 magazine advertisement offered to sell Hoosier cabinets direct from the factory with prepaid freight "East of the Mississippi and North of Tennessee." While later ads encouraged the housewife to visit her Hoosier dealer, a 1910 advertisement in *Good Housekeeping Magazine* mentioned a "Special Offer to women in towns where we have no dealer."

By 1910 The Hoosier Manufacturing Company had sold 300,000 kitchen cabinets and was represented by nearly 3000 dealers. A large Hoosier warehouse was established in Kansas City for western distribution of Hoosier cabinets. In 1916, when the one millionth Hoosier cabinet was sold, there were more than 5000 authorized Hoosier dealers. The company continued to grow and by 1920 two million Hoosier cabinets had been sold. At that time The Hoosier Manufacturing Company complex consisted of five buildings and occupied several hundred thousand square feet of space.

The Hoosier Manufacturing Company dealer organization was tightly controlled by the company. The price that the dealer charged for each Hoosier cabinet was fixed by the company and he was not allowed to sell the cabinet for any more or any less. Also there was never more than one Hoosier dealer in any town. A Hoosier dealership was a coveted franchise awarded only to reliable and reputable furniture dealers. In 1914 one furniture dealer was said to have made a profit of $27,000 alone selling Hoosier cabinets. When you consider that the annual income of the average American factory worker was less than $1000 in 1914, $27,000 was a great deal of money.

Many Hoosier cabinets were sold through the famous Hoosier club plan. According to the club plan, the customer paid a $1.00 membership fee (actually a down payment) and a $1.00 per week dues until the full purchase price of the cabinet was paid. There was no interest or carrying charge applied to the purchase price. A dealer was usually permitted to organize a club once or twice a year and memberships were supposedly limited by the company. In later years the dues were raised to $10 per month.

The Hoosier dealers were aided to a large extent by the aggressive advertising program of the company. They continually ran ads in the most popular magazines and by the 1920s their annual advertising budget had grown to nearly $250,000. The Hoosier Manufacturing Company knew they were the biggest and best manufacturer of kitchen cabinets and they wanted to make sure that everyone else knew it. A 1915 ad in *The Saturday Evening Post* stated: "Hoosier leads the world in kitchen cabinets. No five makers combined can equal our sales."

The Hoosier Manufacturing Company continued to flourish through the 1920s. The Hoosier cabinet was sold internationally and the company had a representative in England. When the popularity of the Hoosier cabinet peaked about 1925, the company employed over 700 people in the factory and an additional sixty people worked in the office. Nearly fifty traveling salesmen called on Hoosier dealers throughout the United States. The average production at that time was about 700 cabinets a day. In the early 1920s The Hoosier Manufacturing Company began the production of porcelain top kitchen tables and breakfast sets of matching tables and chairs.

By 1930 the growing popularity of built-in kitchen cabinets caused the demand for free-standing cabinets such as the Hoosier to decline. In order to remain competitive The Hoosier Manufacturing Company offered an extensive line of built-in cabinets. The company expanded its production of breakfast sets and added dinning room furniture to its line. They continued to manufacture free-standing kitchen cabinets until 1940. However, these newer cabinets were modern in design and bore little resemblance to the classic Hoosier cabinets of the 1920s

James S. McQuinn died in 1938 and his son Emmett, who had served as sales manager and business manager for many years, became president. Continued operation of the company became difficult when World War II created a shortage of labor and materials. The Hoosier Manufacturing Company was sold in 1942 and liquidated by the new owners. The factory building was used as a government warehouse during the war and later used for the production of corrugated boxes. The factory and office buildings have been vacant since May of 1988.

Although nearly four million Hoosier cabinets were produced from 1900 to 1940, the majority were built between 1915 and 1930. Most of the Hoosiers found today are from this period. The 1915 Hoosier featured the stationary flour bin, the pull-out sugar bin, and the revolving spice jar carousel. The 1915 models were available with hinged doors or the roll doors that became standard in 1917. The table top of the 1915 model cabinet was available in aluminum or porcelain.

The same style door hinges were used from 1915 to about 1931. The drawer knobs date back to at least 1905 and were used until 1931. The oval door latches appeared about 1910 and were used until about 1922 when they replaced by the rectangular latch with the embossed "H." Early Hoosier cabinets were built close to the floor with casters that made the cabinet easy to move. In 1921 legs were added to the Hoosier cabinets. The legs were available in lengths of 3, 5, or 7 inches so that the cabinet could be adjusted to the height of its owner. These legs were also fitted with casters.

Most Hoosier cabinets built before 1920 were finished in natural oak. In 1913 the cabinets were available with the interior of the upper cupboard finished in white enamel at a slight extra cost. Models with the enameled interior were called the "White Beauty." In 1915 the white interior finish became standard for Hoosier cabinets. A cabinet completely finished in white enamel was offered in 1920. Although the natural oak finished cabinets were still available, the white enameled cabinets proved very popular. The painted cabinets were actually more expensive than the natural oak models. Beginning about 1925, Hoosier cabinets were offered in a variety of colors. Some of the colors available included white, ivory, citrus yellow, Hoosier gray, spring green, green oaks, and tan oaks. While early painted Hoosiers cabinets were mostly oak, many of the later painted cabinets were constructed of maple or other woods.

The style of the Hoosier cabinet was changed often in the 1930s. The classic Hoosier features disappeared as the cabinets became plain, simple, and modern. The unique Hoosier flour sifter was replaced by simpler sifters including one that was mounted on a upper door. The flour bin door was hinged at the bottom and pulled out for filling. Modern cabinet hardware was used in place of the traditional hardware that had been a prominent feature of Hoosier cabinets for many years. Indeed, these later cabinets produced by The Hoosier Manufacturing Company are often difficult to recognize as Hoosiers. Since the number of free-standing cabinets produced by Hoosier in the 1930s was relatively small, these later model Hoosier cabinets are not as plentiful as Hoosier cabinets produced in the 1920s.

The Hoosier cabinets shown on the following pages include dated magazine ads, illustrations from Hoosier Manufacturing Company advertising materials, and recent photographs of Hoosier cabinets. Most of the Hoosier cabinets shown in the photos have been restored to some extent.

The dates for the Hoosier Cabinets Nos. 110, 141, 151, and 162 have been approximated by comparing these cabinets with Hoosier cabinets shown in dated advertisements. Beginning about 1920, The Hoosier Manufacturing Company used the first two digits of their cabinet model numbers to indicate the year of manufacturer. For example, the Model No. 2154 on the back of a Hoosier cabinet indicates that the cabinets was made in 1921. Although most Hoosier model numbers after 1920 contained four digits, there were some three-digit model numbers.

The dates given for the photographed Hoosier cabinets are only approximate. The Hoosier Manufacturing Company made some of the more popular styles for several years, although there were often subtle differences from one year to the next. Since some of the accessories have often been removed or a cabinet has been altered before it was restored, it is usually impossible to give the exact year of manufacturer unless the model number is still readable. However, these illustrations and photos should enable you to date most Hoosier cabinets within five to six years.

Munsey's Magazine 1906

HOOSIER Cabinet No. 110. Circa 1908. Cabinet was 67 inches high by 40 wide with stationary wood work top. Wood flour bin with tin sifter was first used by Hoosier about 1900. Tin sugar bin mounted on right door. There were four drawers in the upper section of the cabinet. This was the economy model of the Hoosier cabinets at that time.

HOOSIER Cabinet No. 141. Circa 1908. Cabinet was 67 inches high by 40 inches wide and had an aluminum covered pull-out work top. Clear glass was used in the china cupboard doors. Hoosier cabinets of this era had japanned spice cans and coffee and tea canisters. Lower section featured a sliding shelf for easy access to pots and pans. The lower door had metal racks for pie pans and other utensils.

HOOSIER Cabinet No. 151. Circa 1908. This tall cabinet was 78 inches high and 40 inches wide. It featured a pull-out aluminum covered work top, clear glass china cupboard doors, and a sliding shelf in the lower section. The japanned spice cans and coffee and tea canisters are quite rare today.

HOOSIER Cabinet No. 162. Circa 1908. This cabinet was 67 inches high and 52 inches wide and featured a wide aluminum covered pull-out work top. With eight doors and ten drawers, this was probably the largest Hoosier cabinet manufactured at that time. In addition to the metal bread drawer, there were three tin covered drawers located just above the lower storage area.

A Hoosier Model 162 recently photographed in an antique shop. This rare old Hoosier cabinet still has its original finish. Although the flour bin is missing and the aluminum work top is badly worn, most of the original hardware is intact. Considering the age of this cabinet and that it had been stored in a barn for several years, it is in fairly good condition.

The Hoosier Special Contains

More than any other Kitchen cabinet.

Sanitary "satinized" flour bin with sifter attached.

A self-feeding "satinized" sugar bin.

A roomy aluminum covered extension work table top.

Air-tight crystal glass spice jars.

Colonial crystal glass tea and coffee canisters.

"Satinized" metal bread and cake box.

Handy sliding shelf.

Plenty of roomy drawers and cupboards.

And many other valuable features.

What the Hoosier Special Means To You

It will save you time, energy and steps—cut your kitchen work in two.

It will give you more time for other things.

It pays for itself in the waste it saves.

It saves you many weary hours of standing.

It gives you a neat, orderly kitchen.

It is the most convenient kitchen cabinet ever built.

It is a bargain.

Do You Want Kitchen Comfort?

A Postal Card to us will bring a Booklet you really should have

The patented extension work table top of the Hoosier Special when pulled out 16 inches is as comfortable to sit by as the dining table, and it isn't necessary for you to get up for your utensils and supplies every few minutes. They are all grouped around this aluminum covered work table, right at your fingers' ends.

You don't take one unnecessary step or waste one minute looking for misplaced articles. You don't find at the last minute that you are out of salt or baking powder. You keep your supplies right before you. You can see every day just what you need, and you even have a handy Hoosier memorandum to help you keep your supplies complete.

The Hoosier Special is a real, work-saving, comfort-giving kitchen convenience. It saves time by saving steps. It saves you many long, weary hours on your feet, and does away with the back-breaking strain of leaning over a kitchen table hour after hour.

A Handsome Piece of Furniture

To the well-known regular Hoosier conveniences we have added, in the Hoosier Special Cabinet, improvements that are entirely new. The result is a really beautiful cabinet—all the metal work in the flour bin and sifter, self-feeding sugar bin and mouse-proof bread and cake box is "satinized," and sparkles like frosted silver. Crystal glass Colonial shaped jars enhance the charming effect of the mellow finish and ruddy copper trimmings reflected in the glistening aluminum table top.

Over 250,000 practical housekeepers, by giving us the cream of their sensible suggestions, have made this Hoosier Cabinet the most beautiful, useful and practical kitchen cabinet ever built.

It Pays For Itself

And the Hoosier Special is an investment. It pays for itself in the waste it saves.

In a new house it gives vastly more convenience than the built-in cupboards and pantries, at about half the cost. It makes convenient kitchens out of inconvenient ones without the expense of remodeling.

The Hoosier Special is a durable cabinet, and the price is very low. You really get a $35.00 to $40.00 cabinet, but the price to you, fixed everywhere by us, is no more than for a common ordinary cabinet. Write us and we will tell you exactly what it will cost at your home.

How We Can Guarantee You a Bargain

We make more than four times as many cabinets as any other manufacturer—*that means a low factory cost.* We prefer small profits and large sales. Our agents—the furniture merchants—sell in the same way. While their profit on each sale is small, the total is satisfactory.

So, you see, our low-price and fixed-price policy saves you several dollars on a cabinet.

Some "Inside" Facts

Now let us tell you some inside facts about the kitchen cabinet business, and how our low standard price affects the manufacturers of imitations.

They buy material in small quantities and manufacture only a few cabinets at a time, so their cost is much higher than ours. No one will take chances on paying as much for an unknown imitation as they pay for the standard Hoosier Cabinet. So the imitators' selling price must be lower. They must, therefore, do one of two things—lose money or *cut quality.* Decide for yourself which is the natural thing to do.

Here are just a few of the ways quality may be cut:

Imitators may use gum (sometimes called "satin walnut") or elm in place of specially prepared solid oak, costing about twice as much, which is used in the Hoosier. The "copy cabinet" may look as well at first, but it cannot wear.

Zinc may be used in place of pure and sanitary aluminum, used exclusively in the Hoosier Cabinet. Zinc costs 5 cts. per pound, aluminum 85 cts. per pound. We use aluminum because we know it is the only metal that will give perfect satisfaction in the table top. Zinc rust is "oxide of zinc," and is poisonous. Aluminum cannot rust or corrode.

Last Ten Years Longer

Imitators may use single-ply panels, which cost about one-fourth as much as the Hoosier three-ply, warp-proof panels. Both look the same when new, *but the difference in their life is about ten years.*

Resin varnish, which costs 40 cts. a gallon, may be used in place of our special water-proof coating, costing $1.50 a gallon. The cheaper finish looks fine when new—has a high gloss—but its life in the kitchen is short.

There are many other ways of cutting quality without sacrificing appearance, so you cannot tell by looking at a cabinet how long it will last. Only an expert can see all of the places where the quality has been cut. *The unerring guide is the Hoosier Trade Mark.* You take chances when you buy an unknown kind.

When you buy a Hoosier you are assured of a lasting, labor-saving, comfort-giving kitchen convenience, in which the choicest materials have been assembled with the highest skill. You are protected by the permanent guarantee of a responsible manufacturer as well as that of your furniture dealer.

SPECIAL OFFER Before you examine a kitchen cabinet at the stores, it is to your decided advantage to send for our interesting and beautiful catalogue. It is packed full of practical facts that you should know about any kitchen cabinet before you buy. It tells you how you can get one of the comfortable HOOSIER KITCHEN STOOLS (shown above) at a very low price. Write today before you forget. Send us your name and address on a postcard, or if more convenient, tear off the bottom of this page, write your name and address on that, and mail it now.

THE HOOSIER MANUFACTURING COMPANY
Main Office and Factory, NEW CASTLE, IND.
BRANCHES:
428 Lexington Avenue, New York   239 Pacific Bldg., San Francisco, Cal.

←LOOK FOR THIS TRADE MARK→

THE HOOSIER SAVES STEPS KITCHEN CABINET

Half of All Kitchen Work is Unnecessary!

You can cut your kitchen work in two; avoid all the disagreeable part, just as 300,000 women are doing, who are using and praising the

Hoosier Kitchen Cabinet

They did not think it would do it, but after using it they saw the time, steps, labor and waste it saved, three times a day, the comfort of sitting down at its extending table top, the convenience of having everything within reach.

Any woman can be free from kitchen drudgery.

Try a Hoosier cabinet for 30 days in your own kitchen—then decide for yourself.

You will not be content to be without one after you know what we claim is true.

Our terms are so liberal and agreeable that you can own one without ever missing the little money it costs.

Save $5 to $15 on Your Cabinet

Write for our handsome catalogue; it tells why it is easier for you to buy the Hoosier and be sure than it is to buy an unknown cabinet and take chances.

Special Offer to women in towns where we have no dealer.   Write us about it.

THE HOOSIER MANUFACTURING CO., 800 Adams Street, New Castle, Indiana

More Hoosiers in use than all other makes combined.

This restored Hoosier dates back to about 1910. Note the flour bin with the large glass window and the sugar bin mounted on the right door. The jappaned spice cans in the racks on the right door are rarely seen today. The door latches and hinges have been replaced.

1—She Sits While Working   *2—Reaches and Saves Walking*   *3—Through Early — Not Tired*

The Moving Picture Story Of a Hoosier Cabinet

It saves time and strength and health by saving steps and standing.

These photographs were taken in a clever woman's kitchen. She saves many hours most women spend in work.

Note how skillfully she groups her utensils and supplies; the time this order and convenience saves.

She sits while working, thus escaping the tired feeling that comes from being always on her feet.

The Hoosier Cabinet combines her pantry, cupboard and work table in a single spot. Note the miles of steps this saves.

500,000 Such Stories

Now reflect that half a million other women have chosen this woman's way.

Their kitchens repeat her kitchen's story.

And their praises every day are winning other thousands to the Hoosier Cabinet.

Study the reasons they give for their overwhelming approval.

And remember, these are powerful reasons why you should have Hoosier too.

Mark What Wins Them

The Hoosier is amazingly convenient.

Note the splendid metal flour bin with its handy sifter, and the metal bin for sugar at your fingers' ends.

The twelve crystal jars for tea, coffee, salt and spice.

Look, too, at the roomy upper cupboard for dishes and supplies; the cupboard below for pans and pots; the metal-lined drawer correctly designed for fresh cake and bread; still other drawers for towels and cutlery.

Crowning all, note the hygienic metal table, proof against both rust and heat; cleaned without any scrubbing by simply wiping with a hot, moist cloth.

It pulls out sixteen inches farther when you want to use it; slips back when you are through.

Spend an hour with this wonderful machine. Count its labor-saving features one by one. Even then you won't know all of the delights its owners can tell you.

Compare Kitchens

Compare the kitchen of a Hoosier owner with your own. Note the system, the neatness, the order. Consider the endless time a Hoosier saves.

Think what this spare time would mean to you day after day, if you worked sitting down so you could feel rested enough to enjoy it.

The more you compare, the more eager you will be to have a Hoosier. Now see how easily you can own one.

Club Plan in Detail

Here is our famous club plan. Nearly 400,000 of the half million Hoosiers have been sold in this way.

Costs Only $1.00

You merely pay a dollar to the Hoosier agent.

Your Hoosier is delivered right away.

After that, weekly dues are $1.00 until you have completed the low price.

Your $1.00 membership fee counts as part of the price.

Low Fixed Price

We fix the price everywhere to make sure you don't pay too much.

The more cabinets we make the less each one costs. The fixed price gives you all the saving. Comparison will reveal your bargain.

Every Hoosier agent sells at our price. We have only one agent in any town. He is a reliable furniture dealer.

This spring we permit him to organize one club. Membership, of course, will be limited, as we can't supply all who would like to join.

So make your decision soon. Now this month there is a waiting list for 20,000 Hoosiers, and the list is growing each hour.

Don't delay your action until it's too late to get a genuine Hoosier this year.

Get This Book

Write now for the "Model Kitchen Book." It's rather famous in Domestic Science Schools. It shows you practical ways to save work. It is free.

We'll direct you where to join a genuine Hoosier Club. 3000 towns are forming them.

THE HOOSIER MANUFACTURING COMPANY, 135 Calhoun Street, NEW CASTLE, INDIANA

Branch: Mezzanine Floor, Pacific Bldg., San Francisco, California.   Sold also throughout Canada.

Look for this blue and white sign. The furniture dealer who displays it believes in high quality at low price. He is a good man to know.

LICENSED AGENTS FOR
Hoosier Kitchen Cabinets

THE HOOSIER SAVES STEPS KITCHEN CABINET   THE HOOSIER SAVES STEPS KITCHEN CABINET

Why 700,000 American Women *Use* HOOSIER CABINETS

—Save miles of steps
—Save hours of time
—Save supplies
—Save money
—Save nerves
—Save health

From California to Maine you'll not find a town without at least one kitchen made up-to-date by a Hoosier Cabinet. Some entire communities have model Hoosier Cabinet Kitchens.

—Here Are Other Reasons Why So Many Women Buy It:

(1) PERFECTLY SANITARY—Take it entirely apart in one minute for cleaning or a sun bath.
(2) MATCHLESS CONVENIENCE—40 labor-saving features—17 entirely new.
(3) LIFETIME CONSTRUCTION.
(4) YOUR MONEY BACK if you're not delighted.

Women all over the United States praise the Hoosier

You need it, too

The HOOSIER CABINET NATIONAL STEP SAVER For American Women

$1.00 puts *White Beauty,* the New HOOSIER, in Your *Home*

You simply select the Hoosier Kitchen Cabinet you want and pay the Hoosier agent $1.00. He delivers your Hoosier at once. Balance is payable in small weekly dues of only $1.00.

There are no extras to pay; no interest. The low cash price we fix prevails strictly. This price, based on enormous sales, is now lower than that of common cupboard cabinets.

But Only a Limited Number

of Hoosiers are sold on this plan. Each Hoosier agent sets the week of his own sale. You have needed a Hoosier Cabinet a long time. This is an exceptional opportunity to own one without ever missing its small cost. Grasp this opportunity.

Write Now for "You and Your Kitchen"

This 48-page illustrated book tells what you want to know about your kitchen and the Hoosier Cabinet. With it we'll send prices and full information, without obligation to you, free of charge.

THE HOOSIER MANUFACTURING COMPANY, 1410 Sidney Street, NEW CASTLE, INDIANA

Only one dealer in a town sells Hoosiers
Branch—Pacific Building, San Francisco

Highest Award Panama-Pacific Exposition, San Francisco

Now–The National Sale of
HOOSIER KITCHEN CABINETS

Go See This Hoosier Window in Your Town
Save Many Dollars — Save Miles of Steps

This National Hoosier Sale is to celebrate our latest triumph—the new Hoosier WONDER—at $9.00 less than standard price.

There never before was a kitchen cabinet like it for the money. Yet our prices are low. And the reason is this:

World Leaders

Hoosier leads the world in kitchen cabinets. No five makers combined can equal our sales. Nearly a million delighted women now own Hoosiers.

An output like that brings down our factory cost per cabinet. So we pass on this saving to Hoosier users in the form of betterments and lower prices.

Big Surprises

The Hoosier Special, the Hoosier Beauty, the Roll Door Hoosier and the Hoosier De Luxe have long been famous. This fall they introduce new labor-saving features. But you can get them at the old-time prices because we've made them in extra large quantities for this sale.

The Hoosier WONDER is like them in wood, in workmanship and finish. Yet the very low price will be the biggest surprise in years. Ask the Hoosier agent in your town when you call to see these cabinets.

Delivered for $1

5000 Hoosier agents are authorized during this sale to deliver a Hoosier to every woman who pays $1 on the purchase price. Then to accept $1 weekly for the balance of our low fixed price.

We give you this absolute warrant—**"Your money back if you are not delighted."**

So why not try the Hoosier when you take no risk? Go to this sale at once, and see how the Hoosier saves hours of time and toil and miles of steps.

Mrs. Frederick's Book FREE

If you don't see this Hoosier window in your town, send us your name and address. Then we'll mail you Mrs. Christine Frederick's book, "You and Your Kitchen." It discloses many valuable household helps, tells all about the Hoosier Step Savers and how and where to get one. Write for this book today.

To Dealers—

Our 5000 Hoosier agents have the majority of the kitchen cabinet business in their towns. 65 per cent of them have sold Hoosiers exclusively for more than ten years. Last spring they sold $1,750,000 worth of Hoosiers. Dealers say this is the result of our sixteen years' policy to build the best cabinet at the lowest possible price.

We sell through only one agent in a town. Other dealers constantly besiege us for the Hoosier agency, but we already have active agents in most towns. Your town may be an exception. If this window doesn't appear in your town, there may be a vacancy—an opportunity for you. Write us.

THE HOOSIER MANUFACTURING COMPANY, 159 Sidney Street, NEW CASTLE, IND.
BRANCH: Pacific Building, San Francisco

The table is pure aluminum or porcelain—the spotless white cupboards are big and uncluttered by partitions. The utensil tray and deep metal drawers save time. The shaker flour sifter avoids grit and won't wear out. The metal caster sockets won't break. There are food guides, a calendar, pencil holder and scores of little things that make for great convenience.

You can afford a genuine Hoosier now no matter what you thought before. Two new patterns splendidly built like all other Hoosiers have been added as a result of this increased output—at prices amazingly low.

We fix these prices everywhere. They vary a little on account of freight, but a dollar puts a Hoosier in your home no matter where you live—balance in a few $1 weekly dues—and every penny back unless you are delighted.

Write to us today for the price of a Hoosier set up in your own kitchen. We will give you the name of the nearby Hoosier agent without obligating you in any way.

FREE ! To those who write at once we will also send free copy of Mrs. Christine Frederick's famous book of kitchen helps, "You and Your Kitchen." Write today.

HOOSIER MFG. CO., 5111 Sidney St., NEW CASTLE, IND.
Branch: Pacific Building, San Francisco   5000 Agents in United States and Canada

The Saturday Evening Post November 20, 1915

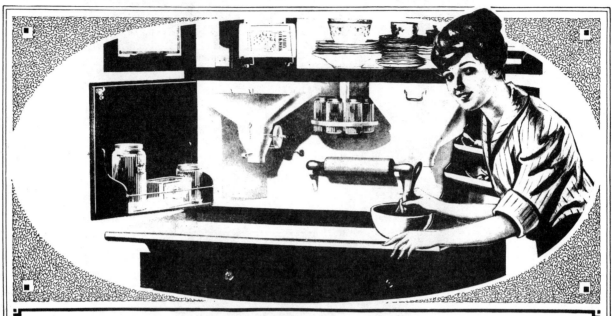

Roll doors may be had if preferred

Don't Spend *Your Strength* in Saving the Price of a HOOSIER!

Women so often feel that it is economy to do without labor-saving equipment that they try to save the small price of a Hoosier, when a few dollars, thus invested, will systematize kitchen work so that it can be done easily and in half the time.

The new Hoosier is a wonderful centralized storehouse that has places for 400 articles, all within arm's reach. Competitors have copied a few Hoosier conveniences, but 17 of these special features can't be found in all other cabinets combined. The Hoosier embodies special ways of saving work that domestic science experts have discovered.

The Important Section of Your Cabinet

The picture above shows the section of your cabinet that is most important—the part that makes it a real helper. Storage space is above and below; the articles most often used are placed where they are most easily reached. There is plenty of unhampered room above and around the aluminum (or porcelain) work-table. There are no useless little partitions to chop up the space and leave no room for work. Your cabinet must have big table space to work on. The Hoosier gives it.

Six exclusive Hoosier features you must have:

1—The all-metal glass front flour bin—easy to fill—easy to clean—no springs or mechanical devices to stick or get out of order.

2—The gear-driven shaker flour sifter which is attached to the bin—sifts flour four times as fast as any ordinary sifter—makes flour light and fluffy—absolutely sanitary—can not grind grit or dirt through sieve—fully covered by Hoosier patents.

3—Scientific arrangement—articles needed most frequently easiest reached.

4—Revolving caster (shown in center of illustration) that brings the spice you want to your fingers' ends in an airtight, neatly labeled crystal glass jar—the final touch of convenience.

5—The ingenious, big-capacity sugar bin—holds more than twice as much as most other bins—and is the only one in which it is equally convenient to scoop sugar from the top or draw it from a spout at the bottom.

6—Finally, doors with a handy tray that holds small utensils, or your choice of rolling doors.

Prices and Terms

Over 1,000,000 women use Hoosier Kitchen Cabinets. Enormous output makes possible our low prices, which now range from $12.75 to $52.50, according to design, equipment and your location. Have the Hoosier delivered at once on our money-back guarantee. You may pay for it a little at a time if you wish, without extra cost or interest. And regardless of the room in your kitchen, there's a special Hoosier model to fit, at a price you can easily afford.

Write for Hoosier Book

Send for a free copy of our handsome new book that pictures and tells all about Hoosier Cabinets and how to save kitchen work. We will also tell you where you can see the Hoosier and have it demonstrated, without placing yourself under the slightest obligation. Think of the miles of steps and the hours of extra work you will save if you seize this offer at once. Write today without fail.

THE HOOSIER MANUFACTURING COMPANY, 1613 Sidney Street, New Castle, Ind.

BRANCH: 1067 Market Street, San Francisco, California

(347)

Hoosier's Council of Kitchen Scientists

MRS. CHRISTINE FREDERICK
Noted Household Efficiency Authority, New York

MRS. FRANK AMBLER PATTISON
Domestic Efficiency Engineer, New Jersey

MRS. JANET McKENZIE HILL
Principal, Summer School of Cookery, New Hampshire

"Hoosier Beauty"

Hoosier's Council of Kitchen Scientists

MRS. ALICE R. DRESSER
Consultant of Household Administration, Massachusetts

MISS ALICE BRADLEY
Principal, Miss Farmer's School of Cookery, Massachusetts

MRS. NELLIE KEDZIE JONES
Household Consultant, Wisconsin

MISS FAY KELLOGG
Household Science Architect, New York

MRS. H. M. DUNLAP
Domestic Science Specialist and Lecturer, Illinois

These Talented Women Will Help in Your Kitchen—Through the Hoosier Cabinet

Hoosier's Council of Kitchen Scientists are among the most capable authorities in the whole domain of household economics.

They skilfully experiment with Hoosier Cabinets in their scientific kitchens and laboratories. And thus they devise unequaled features for saving you time and labor in your kitchen.

Single-handed these experts could serve but few women. Working through us, their helps and ingenuity are open to every home.

New Kitchen Cabinet discoveries which some of these specialists have made are built into the Hoosier. They give us expert advice for women who own the Hoosier—for those who have bought it, as well as those who will. Some plan entire kitchens.

Lifetime Convenience

Not a dollar is added to the regular price. And you can secure the Hoosier on easy terms. Here are 40 work-reducing features that save you hours of time and miles of steps.

Within arm's reach are places for 400 articles. Our experts have planned each section scientifically—the most used things will be closest at hand. Hoosier makes use of space that in many cabinets is wasted.

Not only is this a cabinet of super-convenience, but its lifetime standard of construction cannot be surpassed.

Hoosier Cabinets fit every size of kitchen.

Surprising Prices

More women buy the Hoosier than any other five makes combined. Thus enormous output cuts manufacturing costs in many ways.

So, notwithstanding the many extras you get in Hoosier, the prices are as low as any—$15.25 to $54.50, according to design, equipment, and your location.

You can pay as convenient—a small amount weekly. *Your money all back if you are not delighted.*

Send for Kitchen Book FREE

Our experts have planned six labor-saving kitchens. They are pictured and described in the Hoosier Book—"New Kitchen Short-Cuts" together with all the five new Hoosier Cabinets.

Mail your address before these books are gone and we'll send you a complimentary copy. Use the coupon or a postal—send today.

HOOSIER MFG. CO., 1709 Sidney Street, New Castle, Ind.
Largest Makers of Kitchen Cabinets in the World
Important Branches: 1067 Market St., San Francisco, California   The Adams Furniture Company, Toronto, Canada
The Hoosier Store, 368 Portage Ave., Winnipeg, Canada

HOOSIER

Two Million Women Have Voted for the Hoosier

The three drawers shown here are in addition to a large utensil drawer that extends across two-thirds of the cabinet, just below the work table. Each Hoosier drawer provides practically 30 per cent more room than ordinary cabinet drawers.

The easy-sliding, all-metal cake and bread box is equipped with sliding cake tray that allows cakes to cool uniformly.

One of the many unusual features in the Hoosier is the patented flour shaker. In operation, it makes flour four times as fine as an ordinary sifter, and that means better bread and better cakes. It comes apart quickly for cleaning. Every part of the Hoosier Cabinet is built just like the sifter. Easy to use, easy to take apart and easy to keep clean.

TWO MILLION American women have recognized Hoosier superiority and have installed this woman-emancipator in their homes.

These same two million women have helped to make the Hoosier a *better* kitchen cabinet. For twenty-one years they have given us the benefit of their experience with it. Literally thousands of suggested improvements have been offered by Hoosier users. All of them have been tried out in actual use. It is safe to say that every suggestion that has ever been made concerning kitchen cabinet construction has been actually tried by us.

The best are now embodied in the Hoosier. The rest—no matter how alluring they may have seemed on paper—failed under the test of actual use.

There is no place in the Hoosier for anything that does not actually lessen the time a woman must spend in her kitchen—and lighten her work while there.

Let your Hoosier dealer explain these advantages to you. Sit in front of Hoosier's uncluttered work table. See how every inch of Hoosier's unusually commodious shelf space is right at your fingers' ends. Notice how reaching, stooping and standing have been eliminated. Then—when you are convinced that those two million other women have not erred in their judgment—order the Hoosier sent to your home. If you do, you'll have more time for porch breezes this Summer.

THE HOOSIER MFG. COMPANY

MAIN OFFICE, 620 Maple St., Newcastle, Ind.
BRANCH OFFICE, Mezzanine Floor, Pacific Building, San Francisco, Calif.
BRANCH OFFICE, 368 Portage Ave., Winnipeg, Man., Canada

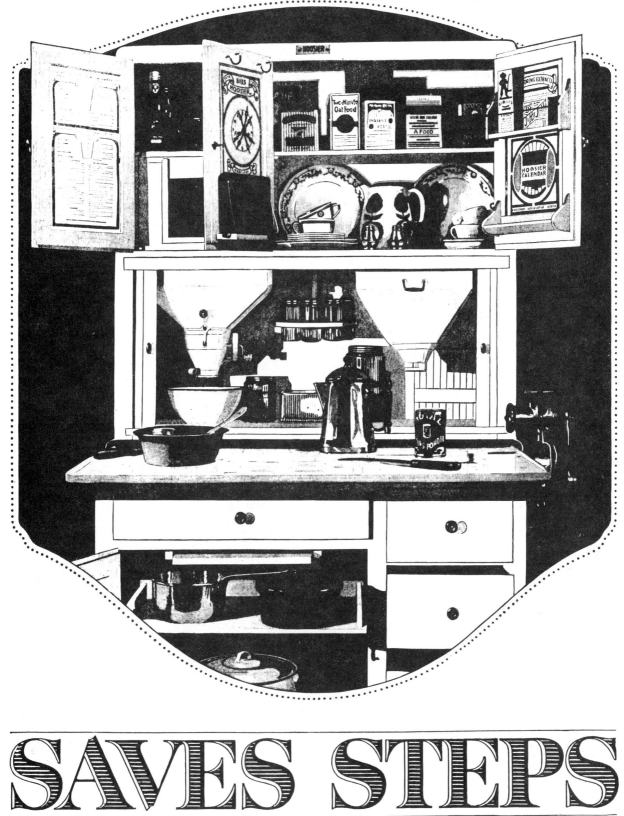

SAVES STEPS

The Saturday Evening Post June 19, 1920

HOOSIER

The Saturday Evening Post September 11, 1920

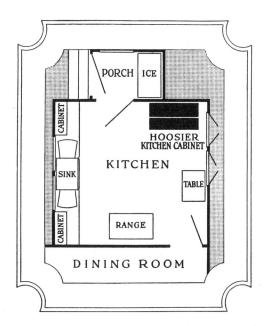

For the Good of All Womankind

THE modern science of home-making is causing thinking women to use more care in the outfitting of their kitchens than they do in the selection of the furniture for their living rooms.

For, what use is a beautiful living room if the kitchen work is so wearing as to prevent one from enjoying the luxuries of the rest of the house?

The two million American women who now own HOOSIER Kitchen Cabinets seem unconsciously to have grasped this basic idea of modern home economics.

They know that the greatest economies they can effect are those of Time and Strength.

And so they have selected the HOOSIER as the logical way to save both.

They know that the HOOSIER is the Kitchen Cabinet of proved improvements. They, themselves, for the past twenty years have been generous in their suggestions of ways and means to make the HOOSIER even better. We can safely assert that every suggestion that was ever made for the improvement of a Kitchen Cabinet has actually been tried out on the HOOSIER. The best have been incorporated in it—the rest rejected.

To-day the HOOSIER represents all we have been able to learn as to what makes a Kitchen Cabinet most desirable.

In it every staple food, every utensil, every movable adjunct to the preparation of meals—and the cleaning up after them—finds its logical place. Each is easy to get at—without walking, reaching, or stooping.

You simply sit before HOOSIER's big, uncluttered work-table and take advantage of the many special features incorporated in the HOOSIER to lessen your labor in the kitchen.

This is true no matter what kind of kitchen you may have—but now comes the latest development for the good of Womankind.

To-day kitchens are actually being planned to fit the HOOSIER. As in the one shown here, and diagrammed above, model kitchens are being thought out in advance, with the HOOSIER so located as to make it the very center of all kitchen work.

In such a kitchen a HOOSIER is at its best.

But—whether you are building a new home or not, you need the HOOSIER—Now.

It can do for you what it is doing for two million other women—save steps, banish reaching and stooping—give you more time for rest and recreation.

Send for our booklet—"New Kitchen Short Cuts."

THE HOOSIER MANUFACTURING COMPANY

MAIN OFFICE—920 Maple St., Newcastle, Ind.
BRANCH OFFICE—Mezzanine Floor, Pacific Building, San Francisco, Calit.
BRANCH OFFICE—368 Portage Ave., Winnipeg, Man., Canada

Copyright 1920, The Hoosier Mfg. Co.

The Saturday Evening Post September 11, 1920

Hoosier Beauty. Circa 1920. This oak cabinet has hinged lower doors in place of the roll doors found on most Hoosiers built after 1917. The cabinet also has an aluminum covered work top rather than a porcelain top. In 1920 this cabinet was available with either a natural oak finish or a white enamel finish.

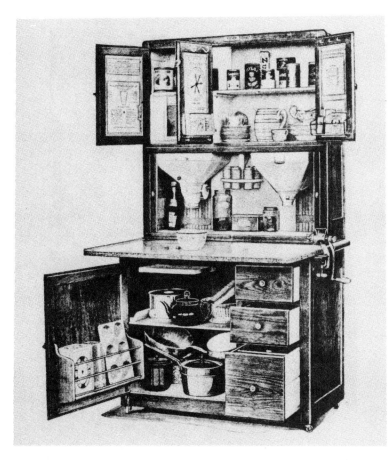

HOOSIER Standard Cabinet No. 2143. 1921. This economy model 1921 Hoosier cabinet did not have the cutlery drawers featured on the Hoosier Beauty. The Standard Cabinet was available with an aluminum covered work top or a porcelain top. It was offered only in a golden oak finish.

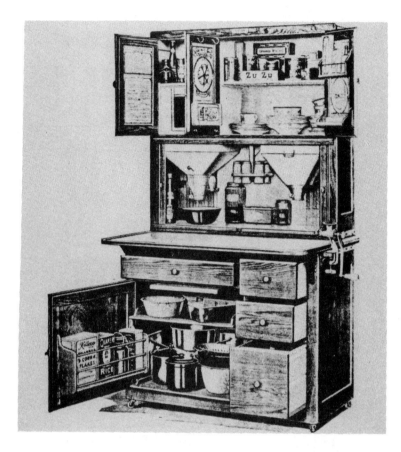

HOOSIER Beauty Cabinet No. 2153. 1921. This cabinet was 41 inches wide and 71 inches high. It was available with an aluminum covered work top or a porcelain work top as shown here. This cabinet was equipped with the famous Hoosier sanitary roll doors. The Hoosier Beauty was available in oak or white enameled finish.

HOOSIER Beauty Cabinet No. 2154. 1921. This cabinet is the same as the Hoosier Beauty No. 2153 except for the hinged lower doors. This was one of the last Hoosier cabinets made with hinged lower doors. The cabinet shown above has an aluminum covered work top. It was also available with the popular porcelain work top.

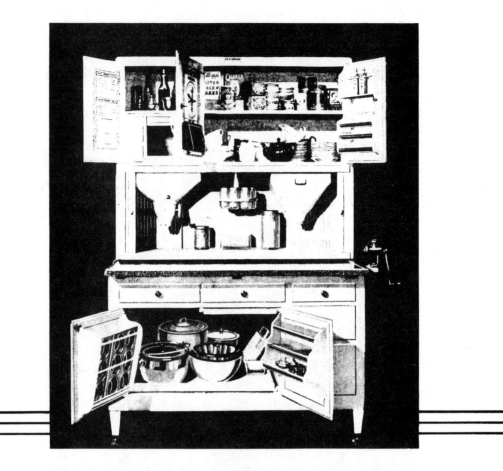

The finest of all Kitchen Cabinets is presented to the American housewife by the Hoosier Manufacturing Company as a fitting climax to our twenty-two years of study of her needs and our untiring efforts to administer to her comfort and convenience. It embodies the best that we have learned from the more than two million American women who have used the Hoosier daily, and who have, in many instances, given us suggestions of inestimable value. Until the needs of the housewife become more complicated, it will be impossible to design a finer kitchen cabinet — this Big Hoosier measures up to present kitchen requirements 100 per cent.

Hoosier Porcelain Tables and Hoosier Cabinets $12.50 to $92.50 f. o. b. factory. See your nearest Hoosier dealer today.

THE HOOSIER MANUFACTURING COMPANY
MAIN OFFICE: 421 MAPLE STREET, NEWCASTLE, INDIANA
BRANCH OFFICES: PACIFIC BUILDING, SAN FRANCISCO; 368 PORTAGE AVENUE, WINNIPEG, MAN., CANADA

The Saturday Evening Post April 2, 1921

Hoosier Beauty. Circa 1925. This is probably one of the most popular Hoosier cabinets built and many are still found today. Prominent features of this cabinet were the three upper doors, the lower roll doors, and the two cutlery drawers below the sliding work top. This cabinet was available in a choice of five finishes including golden oak and white enamel.

The one room exclusively a woman's

And so the kitchen should reflect cheer and charm as well as provide comfort and convenience

The only room in the house which a woman does not share is the kitchen. It is the one room where she may have her own way without consulting others.

Perhaps this is the very reason the kitchen is so often last to get its due. Yet every woman has her dreams of what this room should be!

She would have it furnished as completely and carefully as the family living room—with every convenience to save an aching back and tired feet.

But above all, it would be a *charming*, restful place, with dainty, feminine touches to cheer her work day along.

Don't think that such a kitchen is beyond your means! With a surprisingly small outlay, you can enjoy this convenience, this fresh attractiveness in your own kitchen.

Domestic science authorities have studied your kitchen needs and have designed just the furniture to make it an easy, pleasant place to work. Hoosier Equipment!

First, of course, and the main unit of every modern kitchen, is the Hoosier Cabinet. It is the efficient center from which thousands of households are directed. And it is far from being an extravagance; for you can have a Hoosier on such easy terms you will never feel it!

Next, your need for extra storage space is splendidly filled by Hoosier movable units. One style has deep shelves for dishes, utensils and supplies; the other is fitted as a broom closet. You may use them as an extension of your cabinet or in other suitable places. The units, too, you may have and enjoy on the easiest of payments!

An added touch of cosy cheer is given with the dainty Hoosier Breakfast Set of table and chairs. For breakfast nook or rest corner, it is both decorative and practical.

You can get Hoosier furniture in White or French Grey Enamel, golden oak, or painted to match your special color scheme.

Whatever your choice, you have a tastefully appointed, charming room.

Don't go on "putting up" with shabbiness just because your kitchen is old! New Hoosier furniture will work wonders—and without tearing out or building in! And for *new* kitchens Hoosier is regularly installed as affording more facilities and greater beauty than your carpenter can build in.

The Hoosier Easy Payment Plan will revolutionize your kitchen!

The best part of a Hoosier kitchen is that you will never know you've spent the money! For buying Hoosier furniture is now reduced to the easiest, simplest terms and a very small first payment brings what you need. As you use it you can finish paying in terms to suit your best convenience. The Hoosier store in your town will gladly tell you of this special plan, or write us for details.

The Hoosier Manufacturing Company
925 Warren Street
Newcastle, Indiana

Send for this interesting book on kitchen planning—FREE!

The Hoosier Manufacturing Co.
925 Warren Street, Newcastle, Indiana
British Address:
Ideal Furniture Equipment
No. 9 Preston St., Liverpool

Please send me, free, your new booklet:
"Planning the Modern Kitchen."

Name...

Address...

City...State..........

© 1925, The H. M. Co.

The 1925 Hoosier Highboy!

the greatest value ever offered in a kitchen cabinet, with these new exclusive Hoosier features

New combination glass and wood panel double doors. *Handy metal and wood racks and trays on inside of doors*

New type of flour bin. *Suspended from lower shelf. Accessible; easy to fill. Shaker sifter*

Greater shelf storage space. *Unequalled storage space above. Shelves 12 inches deep*

Genuine porceliron storage drawer. *All porceliron, covered, absolutely moist-proof, dust-proof. Splendid storage capacity for extra flour*

Genuine porceliron bread and cake box. *Just above storage drawer. All porceliron*

Sliding cutting board. *Finest rock maple. Slides over bread and cake box*

Other exclusive Hoosier features. *Spacious white porceliron top, 25 x 40½ inches, on roller spring tension; mouse-proof; ant-proof; shaker flour sifter; 14-piece glassware set; velvet-lined silverware extension drawer; 10-piece cutlery set in extension drawer with compartments*

HOOSIER Beauty Cabinet No. 2762. 1927. This cabinet was 41 inches wide and 72 inches high when equipped with the standard five-inch legs. Several variations of this popular model were made during the 1920s. In 1927 this cabinet was offered in golden oak, silver oak, two-tone gray enamel, and white enamel.

HOOSIER Highboy Cabinet No. 2777. 1927. This cabinet was 41 inches wide and 82 inches high. The Hoosier highboy was made from about 1925 to 1928. The upper section provided about one-third more cupboard room than the standard cabinets. Both the flour bin and sugar bin were mounted beneath the lower shelf of the cupboard section. Since the flour bin did not extend up into the cupboard its capacity was substantially reduced. These tall Hoosier cabinets are rather scarce today.

New Hoosier Designs

HOW attractive! A beautifully furnished breakfast room like this — served from a *perfectly* furnished kitchen, Hoosier equipped! And the beauty of it, too, is that you can easily afford this new comfort and convenience in your own home. For Hoosier equipment, the finest you can buy, is not at all expensive.

Hoosier offers you breakfast room furniture in new designs—oak and enamel finishes in exclusive new color effects. Finishes of *Italian, Wedgwood, Antique, Navajo, Silver Oak* or *Hoosier Grey!* Here are entirely new ideas in beautiful home furnishings. You've never seen their equal.

You'll admire the quaint little Hoosier Buffet, the Hoosier Server's distinctive charm. The handsome drop-leaf table (your choice of *three* designs) easily serves four people. The Windsor-back chairs, gracefully turned, are sturdily built for real comfort.

See these pieces at your nearest Hoosier dealer's. And be *sure* to have him show you the Hoosier Kitchen Cabinet's wonderful completeness. You can well appreciate how its many conveniences will simplify your work, will give you new leisure, new freedom.

Hoosier's liberal credit plan has benefited thousands. A small down payment delivers for immediate use any piece you choose—the balance on easy terms. Your own Hoosier dealer will gladly answer any questions.

Here's a real *working center with everything handy.* The storage units shown with this Hoosier Beauty may be used independently or with any other Hoosier model you decide upon

Note the beautiful lines of this rounded, drop-leaf model —the decorative two-tone medallion center and trim

An invaluable household aid— combination Stepladder-Stool. As a stool—just the right height for all kitchen work. Turned on end —a firm, rubber-cleated ladder

FURNISHING THE MODERN KITCHEN AND BREAKFAST ROOM

FREE—These interesting new booklets. Practical suggestions for every woman who loves a beautiful home. Mail the coupon for your copies

The Hoosier Manufacturing Co.
1027 Broad Street, Newcastle, Indiana
British Address: Louis Matthews
Hoosier Store, 3/5 Preston St., Liverpool
Please send me, free, your newest booklets on Hoosier Kitchen and Breakfast Room Furniture.

Name ....

Street..

City....................................State............
© 1927, The Hoosier Manufacturing Company

HOOSIER

THE WORKING CENTER IN 2,000,000 KITCHENS

HOOSIER'S
SENSATIONAL

75 PIECES

CHOICE
OF FIVE
COLOR
SCHEMES

The
NEW HOOSIER BEAUTY
with
colored glassware & dishes

GROUP OFFER

ONLY A SMALL PAYMENT DOWN

HOOSIER'S unlimited buying power and the co-operation of two great manufacturers and hundreds of Hoosier dealers have made possible the greatest values ever offered in high-grade kitchen equipment

Sometime between now and Christmas a Hoosier dealer in nearly every community will feature the new Hoosier Beauty Cabinet—choice of five color combinations—and with it a beautiful 46-piece golden maize dinner set, a 19-piece set of jade green glassware and a 10-piece crystal set of kitchen glassware—a group offer—all for a small payment down.

Take advantage of this money-saving opportunity as soon as it is announced by your Hoosier dealer. His stocks of dishes and glassware are limited for this special sale.

Here is what a small payment brings you—The New Hoosier Beauty

This New Hoosier Beauty is completely equipped with Hoosier's famous conveniences that save needless steps and labor. It will bring more pleasure to your kitchen work, greater leisure for outside interests.

You have a choice of five smart finishes—Silver or Golden Oak, White, Wedgwood or Grey Enamel. Cupboard interiors are finished in scarlet, apple green, orange or robin's egg blue. Doors are attractively decorated to match.

Golden Maize Dinner Set—46 pieces

Unique and charming is this new golden maize dinnerware, decorated in a beautiful nasturtium design in colors blending with the rich, golden tone of the ware.

Sparkling Jade Green Glassware— 19 pieces

A smart note of color is added to your table with this beautiful set. Glasses, goblets, sherbets and jug have the fluting now so popular. Note the charming design of every piece.

Crystal Kitchen Set—10 pieces

This set consists of seven handy spice jars for your Hoosier's revolving caster and three useful containers for coffee, tea and salt. It is a practical set that every woman will appreciate.

Watch for the announcement of your nearest Hoosier dealer, or better still, write us for the dealer's name and sale date.

FREE—*these beautiful booklets*

Two booklets reproducing the complete line of Hoosier Kitchen and Breakfast Room Furniture in actual colors are free for the asking. Just mail the coupon

HOOSIER

THE WORKING CENTER IN 2,000,000 KITCHENS

The Hoosier Manufacturing Co.,
1127 Sidney Street,
New Castle, Ind.
British Address: Louis Matthews,
Hoosier Store, 3/5 Preston St., Liverpool.
Please send me, free, your two newest booklets on Hoosier Kitchen Equipment and Breakfast Room Furniture.

Name..

Street..

City...State..............
© 1927, The Hoosier Manufacturing Company

Hoosier Highboy cabinet. Circa 1927. This restored Hoosier Highboy cabinet is in very good condition except that the flour bin and sugar bin are missing. The 82-inch cabinets were only in production three or four years and they are fairly rare today. The upper section with the glass panels could be used as a china cabinet.

Electrified HOOSIER DeLuxe No. 2958. 1929. This cabinet was 40 inches wide and 72 inches tall when equipped with standard 5-inch legs. The cabinet featured an electric light at the top and a triple outlet for appliances. The base of this cabinet had two large metal drawers for bread and cakes, a cutlery drawer, and a linen drawer. The wide storage area at the bottom featured a sliding shelf for easy access to pots and pans.

HOOSIER Step Saver No. 306. 1930. This is one of the few Hoosier cabinets made with a roll-up door. The flour bin was mounted on the upper left door which tilted forward for filling. Accessories included a glass sugar jar and a six-piece spice jar set. This cabinet was 69 inches high and 40 inches wide. Available finishes included gray enamel, spring green, old ivory, and a two-tonespring green with ivory.

HOOSIER Junior No. 3037. 1930. This economy Hoosier cabinet was 72 inches high and 36 inches wide. It had a small pull-out flour bin, a glass sugar jar, and a five-piece spice jar set in a metal rack. The cabinet featured a metal bread and cake drawer, a sliding wire rack in the lower storage section, and a pan rack on the lower door. The finishes available included golden oak, spring green, gray enamel, and old ivory.

HOOSIER Special No. 3043. 1930. This cabinet was 72 inches high with standard legs and 40 inches wide. This model had most of the Hoosier features except the two cutlery drawers below the sliding work top. It was available in golden oak, gray enamel, spring green, and old ivory with stenciling on the upper doors.

The Saturday Evening Post May 16, 1931
This unusual Hoosier cabinet featured a roll-up door.

This Hoosier cabinet from about 1935 is exhibited at the Henry County Historical Society in New Castle, Indiana. Note the flour bin mounted in the center of the cabinet and the unusually short roll doors.

3

Sellers Cabinets

After The Hoosier Manufacturing Company, the G.I. Sellers & Sons Company was the second largest manufacturer of early kitchen cabinets. The G.I. Sellers Company was founded at Kokomo, Indiana in 1888 by George Ira Sellers. The company began with about 30 employees and specialized in oak furniture such as tables, chifforobes, and kitchen cupboards. The company gained a reputation for building good furniture and it grew rapidly. By 1905 the Sellers complex reportedly covered more than five city blocks and employed more than 125 men.

In 1905 the Sellers Company was destroyed by a disastrous fire. Ray Striker, a grandson of G.I. Sellers, remembers his mother telling him that the fire had been so intense that melted hammer heads were found in the rubble. Although everything had been destroyed by the fire, George Sellers decided to rebuild immediately. However, Mr. Sellers learned that the factory building of the former Elwood Furniture Company in Elwood, Indiana was for sale. In order to resume production as quickly as possible, George Sellers purchased the former Elwood Furniture factory and moved his company to Elwood, about 30 miles southeast of Kokomo.

After moving to Elwood, two of Mr. Sellers sons, Wilfred and George L., joined their father in the business and the company name was changed to G.I. Sellers & Sons. All of the machinery had been removed from the Elwood Furniture factory before it was sold to Sellers. The Sellers Company decided to specialize in kitchen cabinets and tables at their new facility. They installed new machinery and equipment in the Elwood factory, including some machines specially built for production of Sellers cabinets. Almost immediately Sellers began expanding the facility at Elwood. By 1920 the G.I. Sellers & Sons complex had 230,00 square feet of floor space and covered several city blocks.

George Ira Sellers died in 1909 and Wilfred Sellers became president of G.I. Sellers & Sons. Wilfred Sellers was a very able businessman and the company prospered under his guidance. He realized the importance of advertising and he initiated a program of national advertising in popular magazines of the day. He also invented the "ant-proof caster" which consisted of a stamped metal cup just above the caster wheel. The cup was filled with water or oil which prevented ants from getting to foods stored in the cabinet.

The aggressive advertising program at Sellers was supplemented by a very strong dealer network. At the peak of its operations in the 1920s, the G.I. Sellers & Sons Company had more than 4500 dealers nationwide. The company employed 48 salesmen who called on dealers throughout the United States. Nationally advertised sales promotions for Sellers cabinets were held two or three times a year. During these sales promotions it was not unusual for entire trains of 90 or more cars to leave the Sellers factory loaded with kitchen cabinets and tables.

While attending a furniture show in North Carolina in 1924, Wilfred Sellers' wife contracted typhoid fever. Wilfred Sellers returned to Elwood to attend to business but Mrs. Sellers was too ill to travel. After returning home, Wilfred Sellers also became ill with typhoid and died. Mrs. Sellers survived and returned to Elwood where she lived for about five years before moving to California. When Wilfred Sellers died, his brother, George L. Sellers, became president of G.I. Sellers & Sons. George Sellers remained with the company until 1934.

Most of the workers at Sellers were paid by the piecework method and they received a standard rate for each piece of work that they completed. Wilfred Sellers was a honest employer and the workers were fairly compensated for their work. However, in the early 1920s a Frenchman by the name of Bedeaux, famous for the Bedeaux "timestudy" system, descended on the Sellers factory. According to Charles Short, a longtime Sellers employee, Bedeaux "went around to every job and made it impossible to make ordinary wages, let alone any bonus." Finally, Bedeaux went into the work area of John Conwell to study his job. The elderly Conwell, father of Sellers designer Bill Conwell, chased Bedeaux with a scoop shovel into the office of Wilfred Sellers. Apparently, this was the end of "timestudy" at Sellers.

The Sellers cabinets included many innovations contributed by Bill Conwell who was the chief designer at Sellers. Some of these innovations included the roll-up doors, metal bread drawers, and the flour bin that could be pulled down to waist level for easy filling. The early Sellers kitchen cabinets were built almost entirely of oak by skilled cabinetmakers. After the cabinets were finished they were hand rubbed with oil and pumice to provide a very smooth and durable finish. Some of the deluxe models included etched glass in the upper doors. Narrow strips of slag glass were also used in the upper doors of some Sellers cabinets

We have not been able to find any authenticated photographs or illustrations of Sellers cabinets made prior to 1916. We have been told that the early Sellers cabinets made at

Elwood had maple work tops. A little later the work tops were covered with nickel or galvanized metal. The first Sellers cabinets with porcelain work tops appeared about 1915. About the same time Sellers started using glass knobs for their drawers. The early glass knobs had large glass threads which screwed into a threaded hole in the drawer. The glass thread was a weak point of these knobs and they broke rather easily. It is not unusual to still find Sellers cabinets with the threaded glass knobs. Sellers later used a glass knob with a screw through the center. Glass knobs were used on Sellers cabinets through the early 1930s.

One of the most common methods of identifying cabinets is by the hardware such as hinges or latches. However, Sellers used several styles of hinges and latches from the midteens until they ceased operations in 1950. For this reason, there is very little exact replacement hardware available for Sellers cabinets today. One method used to identify Sellers cabinets is the side brackets used to attach the top section to the base unit. Sellers used the same brackets from about 1910 to the early 1930s. An original Sellers side bracket is shown in the *Restoring Hoosier Cabinets* section of this book. Another characteristic feature found on many Sellers cabinets is the large "Automatic-Lowering" flour bin which dropped down to the work top level for easy filling. Several Sellers magazine advertisements dating from 1916 to 1932 have been included here. These ads should prove helpful in identifying Sellers cabinets. We have also included a photograph of an early kitchen cabinet which, according to the owner, was made by Sellers. However, we have no way of authenticating this cabinet as a Sellers.

Until about 1914 all Sellers cabinets were hand-rubbed natural oak finished. In 1914 Sellers offered white enameled cabinets which were also made of oak. A resin was rubbed into the open oak grain and then rubbed off with wet seaweed to produce a perfectly smooth surface so that the cabinets could be enameled. This process was abandoned after a couple of years and the enameled cabinets were built from gumwood, magnolia, and other woods. Sellers continued to sell natural oak finished cabinets. However, the interiors of the upper section of the oak cabinets were also enameled white starting about 1915.

In 1921 Sellers introduced a new model called the "Majestic." This 48-inch wide cabinet was 81 inches tall and offered about 20 percent more cupboard space than previous 48-inch wide models. In addition to the usual flour bin, the Majestic also had four metal bins which tilted forward. Although one of these bins was apparently for sugar, we are not quite sure of the intended purpose for the other three. Possibly one was used for coffee and another for tea. The Majestic was offered only in white enamel. We cannot find any mention of the Majestic in ads after 1921. The cabinet was probably too large and too expensive to be widely accepted. For this reason the Sellers Majestic is rarely seen today.

Another cabinet introduced in 1921 was the Sellers Mastercraft. This cabinet was 48 inches wide and 70 inches tall. The Mastercraft had a larger flour bin than the Majestic and a large tilt-out bin, possibly used for corn meal. It also featured a silverware buffet drawer located just above the roll door. The Mastercraft was considered to be the top of the Sellers line and was offered in both white enamel and natural oak. Sellers also introduced a low-priced oak cabinet in 1921 which featured vertical roll doors similar to the Hoosier roll doors. This cabinet had a tilt-out flour bin mounted on the upper left door and a swing-out glass sugar jar. This cabinet only had two drawers in the base section. Because of the vertical roll doors and the tilt-out flour bin, the Model 435 is often not recognized as a Sellers cabinet.

In 1927 Sellers added style and color with the introduction of its new Kitchenaire models. This 42-inch wide cabinet with a roll-up door that spanned its total width was offered in three distinctive styles. The Kitchenaire featured five drawers in the base unit including two cutlery drawers that mounted just below the porcelain work top. Since home baking had declined by this time, the flour bin was somewhat smaller than the flour bins featured on previous Sellers models. The Kitchenaire was available in Modern American, Colonial, and Spanish styles. The Modern American cabinet was white enameled while the other two models had a yellow oak finish. All three models featured colorful stenciling.

Color continued to be a prominent feature of Sellers cabinets into the early 1930s. A cabinet similar to the Kitchenaire without the cutlery drawers was offered in 1930. This new cabinet was available with a shaded amber oak, two-tone green oak, or silver oak finish. Matching side cabinets and breakfast sets were available at extra cost. The side cabinets could be ordered with full shelves or open for brooms.

As built-in cabinets became more popular in the 1930s, Sellers offered a complete line of built-ins including sinks. The Sellers company continued to manufacture free-standing kitchen cabinets, although the demand for these cabinets had begun to decline sharply. They also manufactured juvenile furniture including miniature kitchen cabinets finished with the exactness and beauty of the full-size cabinets. Breakfast sets became an important part of the Sellers furniture line and were made in a variety of styles including colonial sets with drop-leaf tables and authentic ladderback chairs.

World War II caused a serious shortage of materials for Sellers and other furniture manufacturers. Also, a number of skilled workers were lost to the draft and higher paying defense jobs. Although the company continued to operate through the war years, economic conditions finally caused the company to cease operations in 1950. The machinery, equipment, and inventory were sold and the vast Sellers complex was leased as warehouse space to various companies. The entire complex was destroyed by fire in 1964. Only the reinforced-concrete drying kilns and the power house remain standing today.

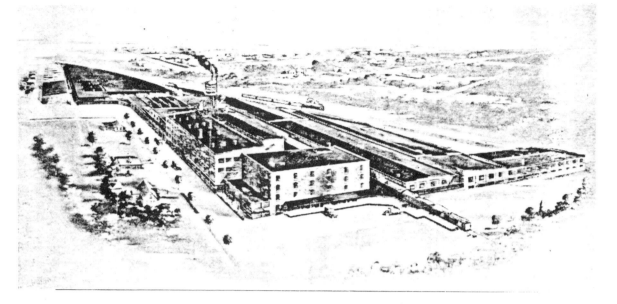

The G.I. Sellers & Sons complex in Elwood, Indiana about 1921. The manufacturing and assembly buildings on the left were four stories tall. This large complex covered several city blocks. Note the railroad spur through the center of the complex.

This reinforced-concrete building that once housed the drying kilns and machine shop are all that remain of the complex shown above. The rest of the former Sellers complex was destroyed by a fire in 1964.

This unusual kitchen cabinet with a pull-out work table is believed to be an early Sellers cabinet. It was probably built sometime between 1900 and 1910. The deep pull-out bin on the right side of the cabinet is mounted on casters and was probably intended to hold a large sack of flour. The deep drawers in the upper section may have been used to hold sugar or other bulk staples. This cabinet was restored by Terry Upperman of Anderson, Indiana as a 4-H project. It won a blue ribbon at the 1988 Indiana State Fair.

This beautifully restored 52-inch wide Sellers cabinet was probably built about 1913. The cabinet is oak and has etched glass panels in the four upper doors. Note the unusually wide drawer above the two doors in the base section. Although the door latches and drawer handles are different from the hardware used on later Sellers cabinets, we believe they are original.

Your Dealer Will Show You

Sellers *Kitcheneed* Mastercraft

and you will find in it

Your Own Idea of What a Kitchen Cabinet Should Be

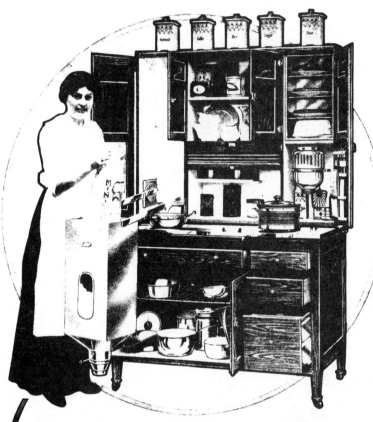

Kitcheneed Mastercraft Illustrating Automatic Lowering Flour Bin

Trade Mark Registered

Sellers Automatic Lowering Flour Bin. A slight pull brings it down over the table top for filling—a slight pressure puts it back into position after filling. Holds 50 pounds of flour—50 pounds that can be placed in this bin with very little effort.

YOU will find embodied in it the necessary space and the necessary convenience features which make possible concentrated kitchen work. Sellers *Kitcheneeds* endeavor to, and do, concentrate such work to the last degree.

You will find the Sellers *Kitcheneed* an ideal piece of furniture—beautifully finished, properly constructed—finished and constructed as carefully and painstakingly as the bookcase in your home. They have an oil hand-rubbed finish making them capable of standing up to the constantly changing atmospheric conditions in the average kitchen.

Sellers ant-proof casters; automatic lowering flour bin; new all-metal bread and cake box; sanitary guaranteed porceliron table top; sanitary glass sugar, spice, tea and coffee jars; afford ample room for all necessary ingredients and utensils essential to the preparation of all meals.

If you will become but slightly familiar with Sellers *Kitcheneeds* through our book, "Your Kitchen Cabinet," or by seeing them at your dealer's, you will at once understand why they have earned this phrase, "Your own idea of what a kitchen cabinet should be."

Sellers *Kitcheneeds* will conserve your strength to a remarkable degree.

And, now then, go to your dealer's, see and examine a *Kitcheneed*—operate the things we've told you about here, then you will realize fully that in *Kitcheneed* "Mastercraft" you have the Kitchen Cabinet ideal.

G. I. Sellers & Sons Company

1001 Thirteenth Street   Elwood, Indiana

Illustrating "Sellers" *Kitcheneed* "Special" with
Automatic Lowering Flour Bin

Sellers
THE BETTER KITCHEN CABINET
KITCHENEED

We wish it were possible to pen-picture all that
"Sellers" *Kitcheneed* will do for you when we say—

"Sellers" *Kitcheneed* "Special" Helps Lighten Your Burden of Kitchen Work Every Single Day

WE would picture you first as we have
shown our girl in the illustration
above—with ease putting fifty pounds of
flour into the lowered bin and then with
ease putting the bin back into position.
We would picture you comfortably sitting
on a stool at this splendid piece of furniture preparing a daily meal.

With that snowy-white, sanitary, porceliron, absolutely indestructible table top
fully extended, sitting there with pots and
pans, knives and forks, all needed utensils

right there just where you want them, and there
with flour, sugar, spices, extracts—every necessary ingredient—not moving one single step—
you prepare that meal.

And then with this picture in mind, go to your
dealer's and yourself operate this automatic lowering flour bin and then sit as we have pictured
you before "Sellers" *Kitcheneed* and come to a
realization of the full meaning of what we say,
"It helps lighten the burden of kitchen work
every single day."

In the meantime may we send you our book, "Your Kitchen
Cabinet"? It tells an interesting story of *Kitcheneeds*.

G. I. SELLERS & SONS COMPANY, 1002 THIRTEENTH STREET, ELWOOD, INDIANA

The Saturday Evening Post December 9, 1916

15 Labor-Saving Conveniences Women Have Always Wanted

No Other Cabinet Combines All These Star Features

No. 1—Automatic Lowering Flour Bin

No. 2—Automatic Base Shelf Extender in lower cupboard

No. 3—Ant-proof Casters

No. 4—Gravity Door Catches

No. 5—Porceliron Work Table

No. 6—Dovetailed Joints and Rounded Corners

No. 7—False Top in Base—Dust Proof

No. 8—All oak

No. 9—Oil Hand-Rubbed finish. Withstands steam in kitchen.

No. 10—Full Roll Open Front

No. 11—Roller Bearings for Extension Work Table

No. 12—Commodious Kitchen Linen Drawer

No. 13—White Enameled Interior —upper section

No. 14—Sanitary Leg Base Construction

No. 15—Glass Drawer Pulls

and 32 other features

YOUR every want is anticipated in this marvel of kitchen comfort!

WHY do you buy a kitchen cabinet? Think! Don't you buy it to save work? Of course you do. Then consider carefully the superior labor-saving features of the Sellers "Special."

This new Sellers "Special" has 15 long-wanted features that never before have been combined in any one cabinet. Things which women have always missed; conveniences that eliminate every needless move—every bit of extra work—and make, for the first time, perfect cabinet convenience, are here.

The Automatic Lowering Flour Bin

The first cabinet with a built-in Flour Bin and Sifter was hailed as a Godsend. But lifting heavy sacks of flour to the top of the cabinet, to fill the flour bin, took all the joy out of the convenience.

So in this marvelous new Sellers "Special" we have a new creation—the Automatic Lowering Flour Bin.

A gentle pull brings it down *level with the table top.* Filling is done without effort. Then a little start, *with your finger,* and it swings noiselessly back into place.

The "Sellers" bin holds 50 lbs. Where can you duplicate that?

This feature alone has won thousands of housewives. It's the most important labor-saving improvement ever made in Kitchen Cabinets. *And no other cabinet has it!* We own the patents.

Other Long-Wanted "Sellers" Features!

See how we *save this labor* in the new Sellers "Special"?

When you open the lower cupboard door, our patented Base Shelf Extender automatically brings the shelf out with it. All pots and pans are in plain view. You can quickly select the one you need from where you sit. That's *real* convenience.

Then look at the guaranteed, pure white, sanitary, Porceliron Extension Work Table. It's a typical Sellers refinement—which all women have wanted.

Notice, too, the Ant-Proof Casters—a patented Sellers idea. They positively prevent ants from crawling up into the cabinet. The Sanitary Base Construction!! The Full Roll Open Front which leaves the table free of doors!! The Steam-proof Finish—White Enamel Interior—and a dozen of other features that will delight any woman's heart. Read them all to the left.

Combined for the First Time In Any Cabinet!

The most important of these innovations are Sellers exclusive creations! No other cabinet has them. This master Sellers "Special" is the only cabinet that offers you *all* these labor-saving helps.

This Sellers "Special" is, we believe, the most nearly perfect cabinet ever built. Holds 300 to 400 necessary articles within arm's reach of where you sit at the work table. Every move is anticipated —everything made more convenient and easier than ever before.

And long years of service are guaranteed by the high quality of materials and superior "Sellers" construction.

The quickest way to prove how much more the Sellers "Special" offers at the same cost is to compare it with other cabinets!

Good Housekeeping Model Kitchen!

Illustration shows the Sellers "Special" in the Model Efficiency Kitchen designed by Good Housekeeping Institute and built by the Standard Sanitary Manufacturing Co. The Sellers was selected because it met all the efficiency requirements—a significant honor.

SELLERS
The best Servant

See the Wonderful Automatic Lowering Flour Bin—

No other Cabinet has this long-desired feature!

WERE this the only advantage in the new Sellers "Special" thousands of women would prefer it.

But it is only one of many features that women *want*—only one feature that assures better results with less labor and in less time than ever before.

So important do we consider the new Sellers "Special" that we are going to demonstrate it *nationally* to thousands of women during

Sellers
Cabinet Week
Oct. 1st to Oct. 6th

See your local dealer at this time. Have him demonstrate each feature of the Sellers "Special." Learn all about it! Compare it critically with any other cabinet. Compare the prices. If you do we know you will select this wonderful new Sellers "Special."

During this national exhibition week, the greatest event of its kind ever planned, most dealers will offer special inducements. Some will sell on attractive credit arrangements; others for $1.00 down and $1.00 a week!

Be sure you see this Sellers "Special" before you buy any cabinet. If you don't know the local Sellers Dealer mail the coupon below.

Fully Guaranteed

Sellers "Special"

Has the patented Automatic Lowering Flour Bin and other features listed. 70 inches high on Ant-Proof Casters. 42 inches wide. 38x41 inch working surface when table is fully extended. Most complete Kitchen Cabinet ever designed.

Sellers Cabinets Cost No More Than *Ordinary* Cabinets

FREE BOOKLET
MAIL COUPON

Tells all about the "Good Housekeeping Efficiency Kitchen." Describes in detail the distinctive labor-saving features of the Sellers "Special."

We will also include "21 Inexpensive Meals," prepared by Constance E. Miller, A. D. E. These are menus for a whole week—with recipes and information about the use of inexpensive cuts of meats, etc. Every woman should have this book. Send no money. Merely mail the coupon completely filled in and we will send booklet free of charge.

G. I. SELLERS & SONS CO., 1005 Thirteenth St., Elwood, Indiana

CABINETS
in your House—

Housewives Mail This Coupon!

G. I. Sellers & Sons Co. 1005 13th St., Elwood, Ind.

Please send me, *free of charge,* copy of your interesting booklet describing Sellers Cabinets, and "21 Inexpensive Meals," by Constance E. Miller, A. D. E., and local dealer's name.

Name_____

Address_____

Town_____ State_____

I own a_____ _____Cabinet.

Date purchased?_____

If you have no cabinet check here ☐

Illustrating
"Sellers" Kitcheneed "Special"
With Automatic Lowering
Flour Bin

Sellers
THE BETTER
KITCHEN CABINET
KITCHENEED

This Trade Mark Iden-
tifies Every "Sellers"

Can You Afford to Be Without a "Sellers" *Kitcheneed* "Special" in Your Home?

L ISTEN! How many unnecessary footsteps do you think you took in preparing your morning meal? How many in cleaning up? How many for your noonday meal and cleaning up? And how many at the evening meal? How many steps from cupboard to kitchen table, and how many to pantry? And you do this each day — hard, tiresome work. Then why do it? Why not just "sit," cut out the ceaseless tramping, have more time out of your kitchen and do not be so tired. Go to the "Sellers" agent in your city and he will show you "Sellers" *Kitcheneed* "SPECIAL." He will show you how all cooking utensils, all cooking ingredients are right at your fingers' ends and that you have a wonderfully sanitary, snowy-white, guaranteed, porceliron, extension work table (a great big working surface) on which to do your work.

In the meantime write for our booklet, "The Auto Bin Girl" — it tells and illustrates the complete *Kitcheneed* story. Let us tell you the name of the dealer nearby who will demonstrate "Sellers" to you.

G. I. SELLERS & SONS COMPANY, 303 Thirteenth St., **ELWOOD, INDIANA**

Why Do Women Prefer the Sellers?

MANY women have asked us this question. Many dealers have made the same query.

Why should so many women prefer a Sellers Kitchen Cabinet when there are so many others apparently the same?

The answer is not hard. Any woman who owns a Sellers Cabinet considers it obvious. Any woman who sees this big beautiful Sellers "Mastercraft" model *for the first time* realizes it.

The Sellers "Mastercraft" combines features that women have always wanted—things that no woman would have omitted. It expresses the average woman's idea of complete kitchen service. In thousands of homes it literally "does the work of a servant."

For example, it has the Automatic Lowering Flour Bin. Every woman recognizes in this a most necessary feature. It eliminates the treacherous climbing on chairs, the dangerous lifting and straining when filling the bin.

Then there is the Automatic Base Shelf Extender. When you open the Lower Cupboard door, the pots and pans are automatically brought within easy reach.

You will also notice the clear white *Porceliron* Work Table, a sanitary feature that every woman wants; also the patented ant-proof casters which prevent vermin from crawling up into the cabinet.

In all there are fifteen of these long-wanted features combined in this remarkable cabinet *for the first time*. No other cabinet has them all. Not one could be omitted without being missed.

Women prefer, too, the scientifically arranged design which provides for great capacity and unusual convenience.

This big beautiful Sellers "Mastercraft" easily accommodates from 300 to 400 articles. That means the entire equipment of the average family. There is no overflow for kitchen or pantry shelves. This cabinet holds everything. You can do all your work right at the cabinet. Every last needless step—every unnecessary bit of labor—every wasted moment is saved.

G. I. SELLERS & SONS CO.

1500 13th Street   ELWOOD, IND.

F. C. Burroughes Furniture Co., Ltd., Toronto, Canada
(District Representative)

SELLERS Kitchen Cabinets

"The Best Servant in Your House"

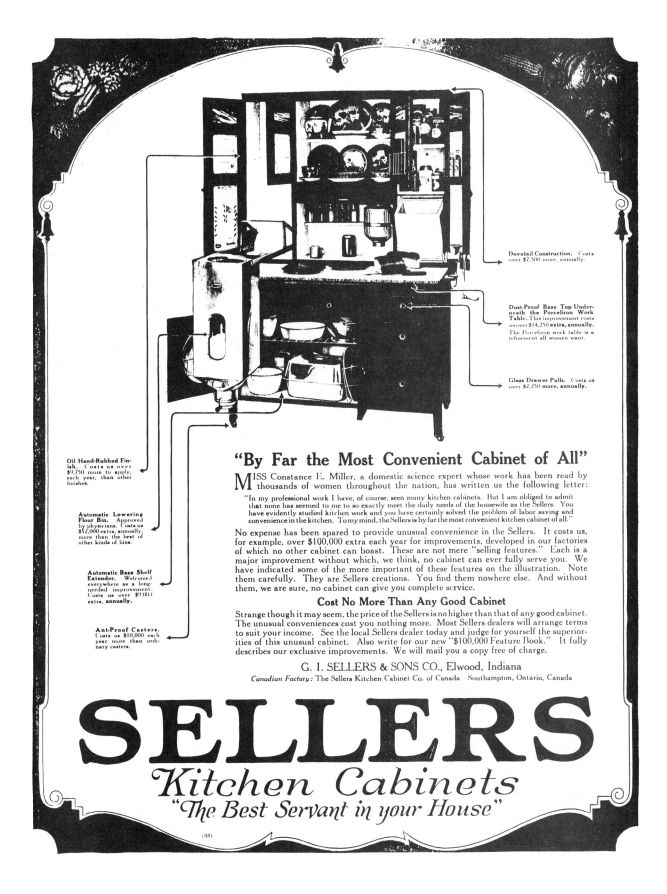

Dovetail Construction. Costs over $7,500 more, annually.

Dust-Proof Base Top Underneath the Porceliron Work Table. This improvement costs us over $14,250 extra, annually. The Porceliron work table is a refinement all women want.

Glass Drawer Pulls. Costs us over $2,250 more, annually.

Oil Hand-Rubbed Finish. Costs us over $9,750 more to apply, each year, than other finishes.

Automatic Lowering Flour Bin. Approved by physicians. Costs us $52,000 extra, annually, more than the best of other kinds of bins.

Automatic Base Shelf Extender. Welcomed everywhere as a long-needed improvement. Costs us over $9,000 extra, annually.

Ant-Proof Casters. Costs us $10,000 each year more than ordinary casters.

"By Far the Most Convenient Cabinet of All"

MISS Constance E. Miller, a domestic science expert whose work has been read by thousands of women throughout the nation, has written us the following letter:

"In my professional work I have, of course, seen many kitchen cabinets. But I am obliged to admit that none has seemed to me to so exactly meet the daily needs of the housewife as the Sellers. You have evidently studied kitchen work and you have certainly solved the problem of labor saving and convenience in the kitchen. To my mind, the Sellers is by far the most convenient kitchen cabinet of all."

No expense has been spared to provide unusual convenience in the Sellers. It costs us, for example, over $100,000 extra each year for improvements, developed in our factories of which no other cabinet can boast. These are not mere "selling features." Each is a major improvement without which, we think, no cabinet can ever fully serve you. We have indicated some of the more important of these features on the illustration. Note them carefully. They are Sellers creations. You find them nowhere else. And without them, we are sure, no cabinet can give you complete service.

Cost No More Than Any Good Cabinet

Strange though it may seem, the price of the Sellers is no higher than that of any good cabinet. The unusual conveniences cost you nothing more. Most Sellers dealers will arrange terms to suit your income. See the local Sellers dealer today and judge for yourself the superiorities of this unusual cabinet. Also write for our new "$100,000 Feature Book." It fully describes our exclusive improvements. We will mail you a copy free of charge.

G. I. SELLERS & SONS CO., Elwood, Indiana

Canadian Factory: The Sellers Kitchen Cabinet Co. of Canada Southampton, Ontario, Canada

SELLERS
Kitchen Cabinets
"The Best Servant in your House"

(88)

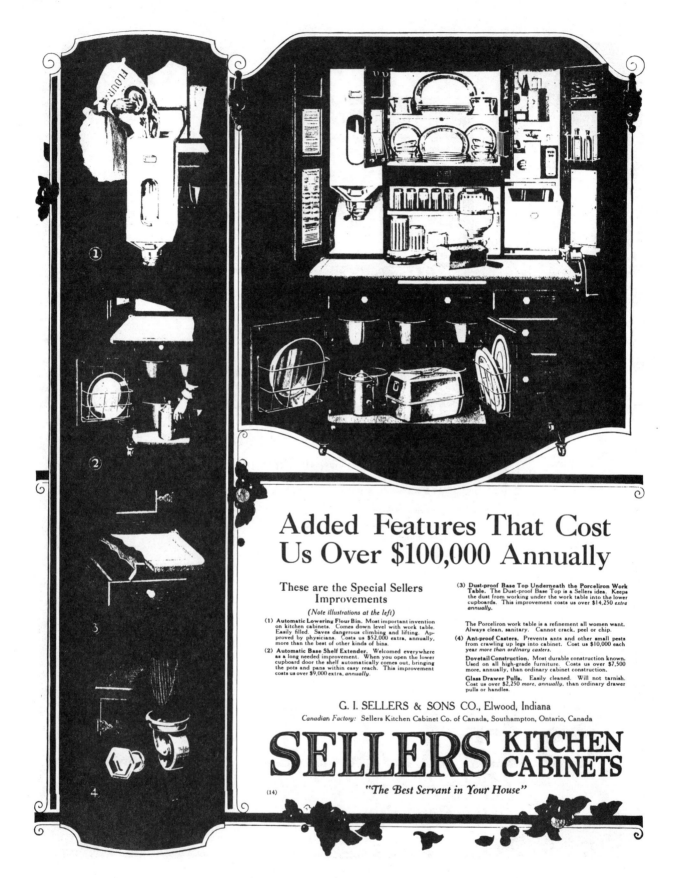

Added Features That Cost Us Over $100,000 Annually

These are the Special Sellers Improvements

(Note illustrations at the left)

(1) **Automatic Lowering Flour Bin.** Most important invention on kitchen cabinets. Comes down level with work table. Easily filled. Saves dangerous climbing and lifting. Approved by physicians. Costs us $52,000 extra, annually, more than the best of other kinds of bins.

(2) **Automatic Base Shelf Extender.** Welcomed everywhere as a long needed improvement. When you open the lower cupboard door the shelf automatically comes out, bringing the pots and pans within easy reach. This improvement costs us over $9,000 extra, *annually.*

(3) **Dust-proof Base Top Underneath the Porceliron Work Table.** The Dust-proof Base Top is a Sellers idea. Keeps the dust from working under the work table into the lower cupboards. This improvement costs us over $14,250 *extra annually.*

The Porceliron work table is a refinement all women want. Always clean, sanitary. Cannot crack, peel or chip.

(4) **Ant-proof Casters.** Prevents ants and other small pests from crawling up legs into cabinet. Cost us $10,000 each year *more than ordinary casters.*

Dovetail Construction. Most durable construction known. Used on all high-grade furniture. Costs us over $7,500 more, annually, than ordinary cabinet construction.

Glass Drawer Pulls. Easily cleaned. Will not tarnish. Cost us over $2,250 *more, annually,* than ordinary drawer pulls or handles.

G. I. SELLERS & SONS CO., Elwood, Indiana
Canadian Factory: Sellers Kitchen Cabinet Co. of Canada, Southampton, Ontario, Canada

SELLERS KITCHEN CABINETS

(14)

"The Best Servant in Your House"

Saves the dangerous climbing, lifting and straining necessary when filling ordinary bins.

This Exclusive Feature Alone Costs Us $52,000 Extra, Annually

SELLERS leadership is not a matter of chance. It has been won only because of the superior service rendered by the Sellers.

Our Automatic Lowering Flour Bin, for example, costs us $52,000 extra each year—that is, $52,000 more than the best of other types of bins would cost us. But see the service it gives.

Instead of having to clamber up on a chair, straining and puffing, with a heavy sack of flour, to fill the bin, you merely pull Sellers Automatic Flour Bin down level with the work table. You fill it with absolute ease. Then a quick movement unlocks it and it slips quietly up into place. This single, long-wanted improvement is welcomed by women everywhere as a godsend. Any physician will approve it.

But this is only one of the exclusive developments which have helped win leadership for the Sellers. Altogether there are 15 important betterments *combined in no other cabinet.*

To supply them costs us over $100,000 extra each year. They have won preference for the Sellers in thousands of homes.

We invite you to inspect this cabinet of super-convenience. Compare it critically. Judge for yourself whether any of these important improvements can be omitted from a cabinet without seriously interfering with its service. Remember, too, that to have these extra conveniences costs you nothing.

The price of the Sellers is not a dollar more than that of any good cabinet having none of them. Your dealer will accept cash or arrange terms to suit your income. Go see him today. Also write for a free copy of our beautiful "$100,000 Feature Book," which fully describes and illustrates the many exclusive improvements of the SELLERS.

G. I. SELLERS & SONS CO., Elwood, Indiana

Canadian Factory:—Sellers Kitchen Cabinet Co. of Canada—Southampton, Ontario, Canada

SELLERS KITCHEN CABINETS

"The Best Servant in Your House"

The Saturday Evening Post April 5, 1920

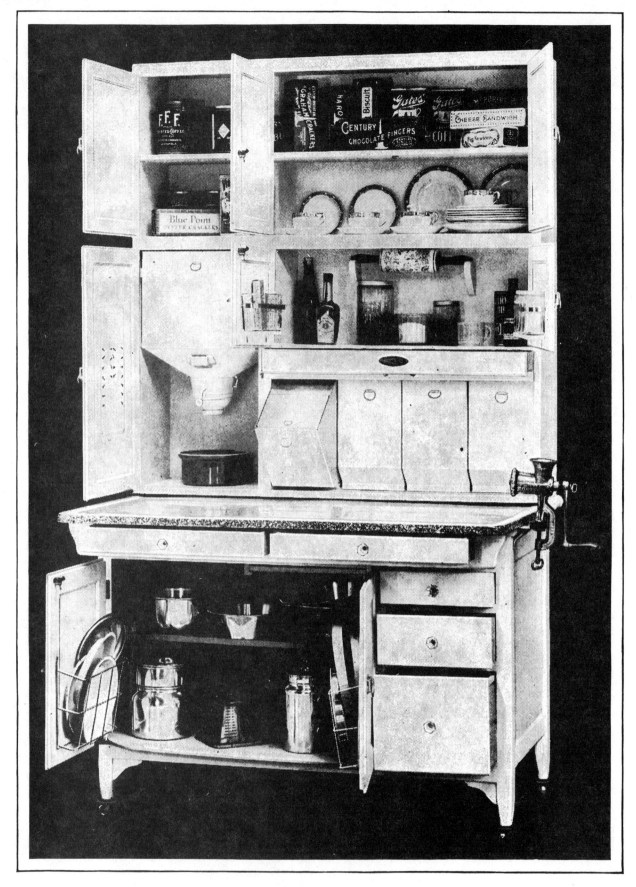

The Ladies Home Journal October, 1921

The Sellers Majestic

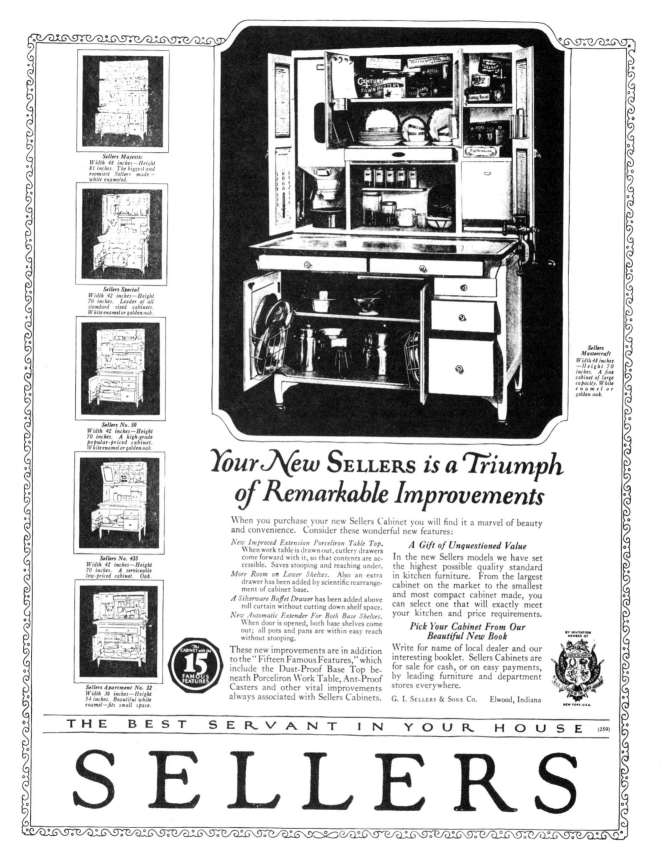

SELLERS 30TH

Send for
The SELLERS
BLUE BOOK
FREE

SELL
THE BEST SERVANT

The Saturday Evening Post May 6, 1922

ANNIVERSARY

To FULLY appreciate how Sellers in 30 years has blazed the way for greater kitchen convenience, you need only seat yourself before one of these beautiful and complete kitchen cabinets.

The unusual ease with which things are done—the many wants, usually ignored, which this cabinet anticipates, will at once be evident. At present reduced prices, and with its many unusual conveniences, the Sellers is undoubtedly the greatest value in our 30 years' experience. Thousands of dollars extra are added to the cost of the Sellers each year, to give you these extra conveniences. Some of them are described below. Read these descriptions. Then judge for yourself if you can be fully served without them.

THE FAMOUS AUTOMATIC
LOWERING FLOUR BIN
—A SELLERS INVENTION

Sellers experts found early in the history of the kitchen cabinet that the lifting of heavy loads of flour, to fill the flour bin, must be eliminated. So the now famous AUTOMATIC LOWERING FLOUR BIN was perfected. This bin comes down level with the work table where you fill it with ease. Then with a little lift it swings back into place. No heavy lifting or treacherous climbing is necessary.

Another feature which women immediately appreciated was the snow white, sanitary Porceliron Work Table.

Women, we found, were complaining of ants and other insects which got into their cabinets. To make this impossible in the Sellers, the famous Ant-Proof Casters were invented. By the ingenious use of borax powder, ants and other insects are effectively barred.

In this same year the first Glass Drawer Pulls were used, because they are more sanitary, will not rust, corrode, etc.

With most kitchen cabinets women found it hard to get pots and pans from the lower cupboard. To overcome this trouble on the Sellers, a device was perfected which automatically brought the lower shelf out as the door opened. This improvement makes it possible for the worker at the cabinet to reach needed pots or pans from her chair, without digging into the dark cupboard. Just recently this has been improved so that now *both* shelves are automatically brought forward.

Dirt and dust frequently work their way in under the sliding top and down into the cupboard of the ordinary kitchen cabinet. So that Sellers users would not be troubled with this, we designed the Dust-Proof Base Top underneath the Porceliron Work Table. This invisible top keeps the inside of the lower cabinet section absolutely dust-proof.

For several years our experts experimented with a finish that would be beautiful yet resist atmospheric changes in the average kitchen. The result was our handsome Oil, Hand-Rubbed Finish, which was applied to all Sellers cabinets beginning in 1905. No superior Golden Oak finish has ever been used.

For greater durability all Sellers Kitchen Cabinets were built with Dovetail Joints instead of ordinary construction.

While Sellers Cabinets had always been made in the standard size, our investigations among hundreds of women proved that many homes could use a larger size more conveniently. It was due to this fact that the first beautiful Sellers Mastercraft model with a capacity of over 400 articles was placed on the market. This is the model shown in the picture —the ideal size for the average family.

Today the Sellers shows the results of 30 years of constant endeavor. Never in all those years have we ceased in our search for practical improvements. In 1920 Sellers introduced the wonderful Apartment Kitchen Cabinet—the smallest cabinet built. This innovation now makes it possible for thousands and thousands of apartment dwellers to enjoy the Sellers. To make it more widely available, the Sellers Apartment Cabinet is made in three sizes: (1) full size; (2) to fit in space under high windows; (3) to fit under a low window.

Another event of importance in this year was the introduction of the beautiful Sellers Majestic, the largest cabinet made. To furnish real convenience in extra large kitchens, this larger size was needed. Therefore, Sellers produced it.

In this past year three of the most important of all Sellers improvements were brought out. One is the Double Base Shelf Extender referred to.

Another is the Extending Drawer Section under the work table. As the work table is drawn out the drawer section comes with it. When the table is fully extended and covered with things, you pull the drawer out and

reach into it just the same as usual. You can always get what you need from the drawer. This is one of the greatest improvements ever made. Alone, it would cause many women to choose the Sellers.

The third improvement is the new Silverware Drawer just above the roll curtain. It is plush lined and a most convenient place

for the knives, forks and spoons in frequent use in the average home.

In addition there is an added drawer and 20% more shelf capacity in the base.

These are just a few of the main features. Many more are discussed in our Blue Book.

A Sellers costs no more than any other good kitchen cabinet. And it costs only about half as much as building-in a cabinet. Besides, no built-in cabinet ever has the many wonderful features of the Sellers. Occupies only the space of your kitchen table.

See a demonstration. Your dealer will gladly arrange terms to suit your income. In the meantime, write for a FREE copy of the new Sellers Blue Book. It pictures and describes all Sellers cabinets and features.   [326]

G. I. SELLERS & SONS COMPANY ◦ ELWOOD, INDIANA
Canadian Branch of Sellers Kitchen Cabinets, Brantford, Canada

ERS

IN YOUR HOUSE

$49 85 for 30 days only

Golden Oak Finish

F.O.B. FACTORY
Regular Price $56.25
White Enamel 58.00
Regular Price 64.50

With the following Sellers features:

Famous Automatic Lowering Flour Bin

Stain-Proof Porceliron Work-Table

Oil Hand-Rubbed Finish on Golden Oak Cabinets

Automatic Base Shelf Extender

Ant-Proof Casters

Glass Drawer Pulls

Dovetail Construction

Roll Curtain

Sanitary Leg Base

If you desire a more elaborate cabinet, ask your dealer to show you the famous Sellers "Special" or "Mastercraft" models.

Illustration shows the Sellers No. 605 in kitchen and climate-proof White Satin Enamel Finish

SELLERS
KITCHEN CABINET

For a 30-day period 5,000 progressive merchants will join with us in a great nation-wide tribute to the June Bride and to the thousands of new homes that will be started during this month.

During this 30-day period the beautiful Sellers No. 605 Kitchen Cabinet, in golden oak finish, may be had at the reduced price of only $49.85 (Regular price, $56.25).

No woman need try to "get along" without a Sellers. Even the humblest kitchen can now have this modern equipment.

Please go at once to the Sellers dealer in your locality. See this celebrated cabinet. Inspect the many time- and labor-saving features it contains. Think how much happier your summer will be when you have this beautiful Sellers to speed up your kitchen work.

But, remember, you must act at once. This special offer is limited to 30 days only. None of these fine cabinets will be available at this low price after the 30-day period. Please see your local Sellers dealer today.

G. I. SELLERS & SONS·COMPANY, *Elwood, Indiana*
Canadian Branch: SELLERS KITCHEN CABINETS, BRANTFORD, CANADA

THE BEST SERVANT IN YOUR HOUSE

ABOVE is reproduced one of the modern efficiency kitchens shown in our book, "*Your Kitchen as It Should Be.*" In this kitchen, designed by the well-known Chicago architects, Schmidt, Garden & Martin, space has been left for a Sellers Mastercraft Cabinet, and the additional storage cupboards built around it.

Among architects of standing it is increasingly the practice to make a Sellers Cabinet a basic part of the kitchen plan. They recognize, as do well-informed builders and housewives, that a built-in cabinet costs practically twice as much as a Sellers, and lacks all those exclusive features that make the Sellers a marvel of convenience—the Automatic Lowering Flour Bin, Porceliron Table Top, Automatic Base Shelf Extender, Extending Table Drawer Section, Ant-Proof Casters, Dust-Proof Base Top, Plush-Lined Silverware Drawer and other features.

Any dealer will show you the Sellers and its "Fifteen Famous Features." Most of them will gladly arrange terms to suit your income. Write for nearest dealer's name and our new book of efficiency kitchen plans.

G. I. SELLERS & SONS COMPANY, *Elwood, Indiana*
Canadian Branch: Sellers Kitchen Cabinets, Brantford, Canada

Floor plan of the kitchen shown above, in which space has been left to accommodate a Sellers Mastercraft Cabinet 48" wide, 28" deep and 70" high.

This is the Sellers Mastercraft Cabinet, shown in the kitchen above. You can see it and other Sellers styles at your dealer's.

SELLERS
KITCHEN CABINETS

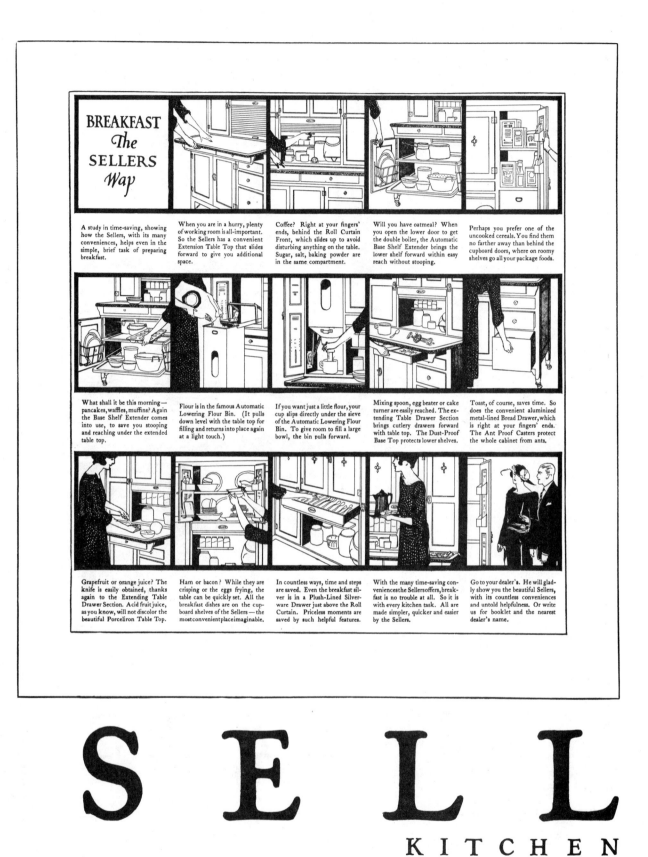

SELL KITCHEN

THE BEST SERVANT IN YOUR HOUSE

If you are building or remodeling, have your architect include a Sellers in your kitchen plan. It costs only about half as much as a built-in cabinet, and offers conveniences that no built-in cabinet can ever have. Write for our booklet, "Your Kitchen as It Should Be," showing six Modern Efficiency Kitchens by the well-known Chicago architects, Schmidt, Garden & Martin

G. I. SELLERS & SONS COMPANY, *Elwood, Indiana*
Canadian Branch: Sellers Kitchen Cabinets, Brantford, Canada

ERS
CABINETS

The Saturday Evening Post October 27, 1923

Sellers Cabinet. Circa 1923. This popular Sellers cabinet was sold from about 1920 to the mid-1920s. The door latches with the embossed "S" were introduced about 1923. The cabinet featured the large Sellers automatic-lowering flour bin and a swing-out sugar jar. However, other features such as the cutlery drawers were not included with this economy priced model. This cabinet was available finished in golden oak or white enamel.

Build your new home to meet the demands of the new day

Foresight! You would not knowingly permit, in your modern home, the doing of important work by methods that belong to a drudging past. Then remember that a modern cabinet is the indispensable working center, scientifically developed for culinary purposes. Plan your kitchen around this logical grouping of fine conveniences, necessary aid to economy and sanitation. You will free your new house from the crudities of built-in shelves and cupboards. if you make a place there for the modern cabinet.

Every home-minded person should be interested in our new booklet

Move the Klearfront in when the builders move out. It is *the* modern work-saver. Scientific preparation of food is made remarkably simple by use of its "fifteen famous features." Cleanliness radiates from the pure white porceliron of its oversize stainproof work-surface, and the "joy o' work" from its superlative helpfulness. Sold by better dealers on terms. Your request will bring our new and interesting booklet "J-8" from G. I. Sellers & Sons Company, Elwood, Indiana. Why not write for it today?

SELLERS
KITCHEN CABINETS

COLONIAL

Klear Front

MODERN AMERICAN

SPANISH

New style cabinets bring *beauty* and *color* into the kitchen

HAVE you sometimes sensed a monotonous, depressing *sameness* about your kitchen?
Other modern women have, thousands of them. In fact that is why we have added to the Sellers line of modern kitchen cabinets and installed units this wonderful

new—stylish—Sellers KITCHENAIRE!

Here you have a kitchen cabinet. But look! It is clothed for the first time in the style, the color of period designs.

Here are gay, artistic effects of the Spanish type! Here are fascinating examples of Colonial and Modern-American (*Klear* Front) design! And each the conception of a distinguished European designer—offered exclusively by Sellers for those whose tastes run to color.

Yet beneath this modern, stylish exterior is the famous Sellers Kitchen Cabinet—the favorite kitchen helper—the time-saver—the labor-saver supreme—in millions of homes.

Nor are these colorful art models high-priced. Every taste and every income can be suited.

In addition there are the beautiful *standard* models of the Sellers—used in millions of homes—preferred by many to whom the pure white, immaculate kitchen is still the ideal.

See your local dealer

At the local Sellers dealer's store you can see the new Sellers KITCHENAIRE. Go by all means. See the beautiful models. Learn the prices. Be prepared to discuss this latest idea.

OUR KITCHENAIRE BOOK FREE
But in the meantime write for our latest booklet—"Apostles of Style." In it are actual *color reproductions* of the new KITCHENAIRE models. There is no charge for the book. Just send your name and address. We will include name of a Sellers dealer near you.
G. I. SELLERS & SONS CO., *Elwood, Indiana*

The SELLERS *Kitchenaire*

Sellers Kitchenaire Cabinet. Circa 1930. This Sellers cabinet still has the original two-tone yellow oak finish and decorative stenciling. A small drop-down flour bin is located behind the left door. The roll-up door spans the full width of the cabinet.

Furnish your kitchen for

**Sellers Kitchen Ensemble
Shaded Amber Oak**

Rich and colorful yet possessing the sturdy strength and wearing qualities of Oak. Ask your dealer to show you the 15 famous labor-saving features. The Utility Closets shown on each side of the cabinet are extra. The Sellers Dinette illustrated is ideal for cozy dining rooms. Table extends. Cabinet No. 30-45 price only $59⁵⁰

SELLERS
KITCHEN--
FURNITURE

Sellers Kitchen Ensemble, Two-Tone Green Oak

This strikingly modern oak finish will retain its beauty to the very last. The cabinet illustrated is Sellers No. 30-45. The Sellers Utility Closet can be had either with full shelves or with space for brooms. Can be purchased separately, if desired. Sellers Breakfast Sets are made in many intriguing colors to perfectly match Sellers Cabinets.

Sellers Kitchen Ensemble, Silver Oak

A genuine Sellers at a remarkably low price. Can be had in many colors, including colorful oak finishes shown on this page. The Utility Closets shown are extra. Come either with shelves for convenient storage or with space for brooms and mops. Breakfast Set matches cabinet in both color and design.

time saving and for beauty
Choose a
SELLERS KITCHEN ENSEMBLE
in the new COLORED OAK

The Sellers Kitchen Cabinet is, of course, the modern housewife's time- and labor-saving champion—a universal favorite.

In millions of homes it is making kitchen work easy—saving needless steps—releasing more hours of each day for pleasure and healthful recreation.

No other kitchen utility in the world offers *all* the ingenious time- and work-saving features of the Sellers . . . a few of which are illustrated here. Please study them.

But Sellers is also the *style leader* in kitchen furniture — sponsor of the modern colorful kitchen and of beautiful wood finishes.

Today the fashion for smartly equipped kitchens is a Sellers Kitchen Ensemble (cabinet, utility closets and breakfast set) in the newest of modern natural grain finishes— *Colored Oak*. A combination of the exquisite graining of this most durable of woods and modern colors.

Two-tone green oak! Sparkling silver oak! Warm shaded amber oak! With all the beauty of the grain retained — and even enhanced — by the use of colors that are transparent as crystal.

If you are refurnishing your present kitchen, or planning a new one, see this smart, colorful, time-saving kitchen furniture at your nearest Sellers dealer's store *at once*.

And do not forget that "Sellers" stands for supreme quality and maximum value; for finest oak and other hardwoods; for sincere, skillful craftsmanship; for the most ingenious time- and labor-saving features.

Yet — because of modern manufacturing methods and volume production — Sellers prices are only a little higher than you are asked to pay for *cheaply built* furniture of no reputation.

Examine these Sellers Ensembles. Units may be purchased singly if desired. Compare the beauty, style, quality, price. See how much *more value* the small difference in Sellers prices will buy for your kitchen.

If you do not recall a Sellers dealer, write us at once. We will send the name of one near you—Address

G. I. SELLERS & SONS CO., Dept. K-3, Elwood, Ind.

We Offer Selling Rights to Dealers

Right now, with these beautiful, new Colored Oak finishes to offer, our National Advertising Campaign and the remarkable merchandising plans prepared for the dealer, the Sellers proposition is one of the best dealer opportunities in the entire furniture and kitchen equipment field.

The Sellers line is, of course, distributed nationally. But there are now some territories in which the Sellers line can be featured more intensively. Your territory may be one of these. Write at once for our 1930 merchandising plans, Advertising Schedule and information about the Sellers franchise possibilities in your territory.

Automatic Base Shelf Extender

As you open the door, the pots and pans are brought out within easy reach.

The Klear Front Idea

Full-width working space. No doors to interfere. No inaccessible working space.

Three-point Suspension Drawers

No jamming. No sagging. Drawers open and close freely from any position.

30-pound Lowering Flour Bin

Ideal capacity for average family. In separate compartment. Easily filled. No muss.

Sellers Kitchen Tables

This beautiful Sellers Table can be had in four fascinating colors. Built with the same painstaking care that marks all Sellers equipment. Notice its gracefully tapered legs. Has compartment drawer with non-tarnishing glass drawer pulls. Fruit juices cannot injure its snow-white porceliron top. Available in three sizes for small, medium or large kitchens. The reasonable price will please you.

SELLERS *Kitchen Furniture*

We're selling Smiles!

AT THE LOWEST PRICES IN 20 YEARS

Smile... and before you know it, you'll begin to get a secret joy out of all this economizing. Take your kitchen, for instance. Today, all thrifty housewives are saving money by doing more baking.

...Hard work? Not in a Sellers-equipped kitchen. Imagine! A colorful, garden-like spot where everything is at your finger-tips...where even irksome tasks are done with a song on your lips. That's a Sellers kitchen ... And you can now have it at the lowest prices in 20 years.

GRINS OF DELIGHT

...will be spontaneous around this delightful breakfast table with its graceful colonial chairs. The table top extends at a touch, permitting a hidden leaf to swing up into place. The restful chairs are built for lifetime service. 32" x 42" closed. 32" x 60" extended. Seats six comfortably. Suitable for the cozy dining room.

SMILE AT YOUR WORK

How can you do otherwise with the finest of all kitchen cabinets to lighten your work and save your time? No other kitchen cabinet in the world offers so much in convenience—or in colorful beauty. Ask your dealer to show you its matchless 15 famous features.

HAPPY THOUGHTS for DEALERS
Never before has the exclusive agency for Sellers Kitchen Furniture meant so much to dealers as right now. Women are spending more time in the kitchen—and Sellers offers them convenience that cannot be duplicated. Write today for details on this business-building kitchen equipment.

MAKE FUN OUT OF WORK

Smile? Who wouldn't in this lovely kitchen with its refreshing colors and labor-saving features? Modernized with Sellers Built-in Furniture at a surprisingly low cost, it offers the utmost in convenience, beauty and compactness. With this flexible unit furniture you can fill in any space or build around windows or sink.

HAPPY HOURS

...will be those spent around this charming colonial breakfast set with its quaint butterfly table and its authentic ladderback chairs. The 5-Ply built-up top can be had in either walnut or maple veneer with base in walnut or maple finish to match.

MORE SMILES IN THE KITCHEN

Wouldn't it be fun, girls, to prepare meals in a happy, modern kitchen like this one where everything is so cheerful and so convenient? Your own kitchen —no matter how old-fashioned it now is—can be easily transformed into a kitchen just as modern and convenient ... at a cost so low it will startle you. How? With Sellers Built-in Furniture. Over 70 separate units enable you to fill in any space. Simple to install. Units delivered ready to be bolted together. No muss, fuss or bother.

Your choice of many happy color combinations. Mail us your kitchen plan today for free estimate on Sellers built-in kitchen.

YOU'LL LIKE IT AND SMILE

... because this Sellers Utility Closet is so useful, so handy to have in your kitchen—or wherever you need extra storage. Can be had either with shelves as shown, or without for use as a broom closet. 70" high. Comes in all colors to match cabinets.

HAPPINESS FOR THE LITTLE TOTS

What a thrill they will get out of this Sellers Juvenile Furniture. For it is not toy furniture, but actual miniature furniture finished with the exactness and beauty of full-size pieces.

JOY FOR THE COOK

...that only a genuine Sellers Kitchen Cabinet with its many time- and labor-saving conveniences can give. This model is No. 3320 and it sells at an unbelievably low price. Has extending *stainless* porceliron work table, 30-pound flour bin, non-jamming drawers that move at a touch and many other outstanding features.

YOU'LL SMILE AT THE TERMS

Cash? Certainly not. Buy on the budget plan —10 per cent down—balance in twelve monthly payments. Your local dealer will be proud to have your payment account on this basis. If he does not offer these terms, we will be glad to place your account through a nearby dealer who does.

Insure more smiles—happier, shorter hours in your kitchen by modernizing it now. Do it with Sellers. For no other kitchen furniture in the world offers so much in convenience. Do it now—at lowest prices in 20 years—on monthly terms so liberal you'll never miss the money.

G. I. SELLERS & SONS CO., *Elwood, Indiana*

SELLERS KITCHEN FURNITURE

4

Napanee Cabinets

The Napanee line of kitchen cabinets were introduced by Coppes Brothers and Zook, Inc. in Nappanee, Indiana about 1913. However, the history of the company and the production of kitchen cabinets by the Coppes brothers started much earlier. The company actually began in 1876 when two young brothers, Frank and John Coppes, joined their brother-in-law in the sawmill business. In 1880 they purchased a box factory and planing mill in Nappanee. Their first products were wooden boxes for a Mishawaka starch company about twenty miles northwest of Nappanee. The Coppes brothers bought out their partner in 1884 and became sole owners of growing enterprise.

The Coppes brothers emphasized product quality and customer service from the very beginning. As a result, their business thrived and Frank and John Coppes soon became successful businessmen. In 1890, Daniel Zook became a partner and the company name was changed to Coppes Brothers and Zook, Inc. Soon after the new company was established, they bought the Nappanee Furniture Company and began the manufacture of home furnishings including kitchen cabinets. Albert and Charles Mutschler joined the company in 1901 as full partners. The company name was changed to Coppes, Zook and Mutschler, Inc. In addition to kitchen cabinets, the company made library tables, dining tables, and other popular furniture of the era. Several of the early kitchen cabinets manufactured by Coppes, Zook and Mutschler are shown on the following pages.

Daniel Zook died in 1913 and the partnership with the Mutschler brothers was dissolved. Although the company was then apparently wholly owned by the Coppes brothers, the name was changed again back to Coppes Brothers and Zook, Inc. In 1914 the Coppes brothers decided to specialize in kitchen cabinets. Their new line of kitchen cabinets were called The Napanee *Dutch Kitchenets*. It is interesting to note that the Napanee line was spelled with one p while the city of Nappanee is spelled with two p's. Since the proper name of the city could not be used in a trademarked name, the Coppes brothers purposely misspelled Nappanee so that they could include it in their name.

The kitchen cabinet business was becoming very competitive and in 1914 the Coppes brothers began a national advertising program to promote the Napanee line. Advertising in magazines such as *Good Housekeeping, The Saturday Evening Post,* and *The Ladies*

Home Journal made the Napanee and Coppes names familiar throughout the country. The company continued to grow through the 1920s and Coppes kitchen cabinets were featured by famous department stores such as Macy's, Gimbels, and Wiebolt's.

Napanee cabinets are readily identified by the famous Napanee Dutch Kitchenet label. Of course, if the label is missing, identification may be difficult for those who are not familiar with the Napanee cabinets. A Napanee cabinet is sometimes mistaken for a Sellers cabinet due to the similarities in construction. However, there are many specific differences between the two cabinets. For example, the slats of the Napanee roll-up door have square edges while the edges of the Sellers slats are slightly rounded. Also, the hardware used by the two manufacturers was significantly different.

The work tops of early Napanee cabinets were made of wood, zinc, or aluminum. The porcelain work tops offered by other manufacturers were becoming popular and, in 1918, they were added to the Napanee line. While early cabinets made by Coppes were oak or elm, natural oak became the standard finish until 1918 when Napanee offered white enameled cabinets in addition to the oak finish. The first Coppes cabinets with metal flour bins probably appeared about 1910. The large Napanee flour bin with the oval glass window was mounted on brackets that allowed it to swing out at the top for filling. The complete flour bin could be removed for cleaning.

Other features of the Napanee cabinets included a swing out sugar jar mounted on the right inside the roll-up door, a rack for spice jars, a metal cake and bread drawer, and sliding wire shelves in the lower section. Most of the early Napanee cabinets used stamped metal bin pulls for the drawers. These stamped bin pulls often help to identify a particular cabinet as a Napanee.

Until about 1928 Napanee cabinets were available only in natural oak, white enamel, or gray enamel. Although I could never understand the appeal of a gray kitchen cabinet, most major manufacturers of kitchen cabinets offered a gray finish during the 1920s. In the late 1920s color became popular in kitchens and Napanee cabinets were also offered in green and yellow finishes. The painted cabinets were often made of popular, gumwood, or mixed woods.

In 1928 Coppes added modular kitchen cabinets to their line. Then, just before the Depression began, the company introduced its first built-in cabinets. The Coppes family managed to keep its factory open during the Depression, although it was necessary to reduce wages and working hours for many of the workers. However, as the demand for built-in kitchen cabinets began to grow, Coppes became one of the most respected names in the business. While the depression years were lean for most businesses and many were forced to close, Coppes continued to receive large orders. By the late 1930s Coppes built-in kitchens were installed in many fine homes and prestigious apartment buildings throughout the country.

During World War II Coppes produced defense related items including gas tanks and bomb racks for bombers, tent floors, and ammunition boxes. When the demand for built-in kitchen cabinets boomed after the war, Coppes again concentrated its efforts on building quality kitchen cabinets.

Although the company is no longer owned by the Coppes family, modern Napanee kitchen cabinets are still being built by Coppes. The showroom at the Coppes plant on Highway 6 in Nappanee, Indiana includes several model kitchens displaying the latest innovations in custom-built cabinets. Also on display is a restored 1916 Napanee Dutch Kitchenet.

It has been almost 50 years since the last Napanee Dutch Kitchenet cabinet was built. Yet, the Coppes company still receives inquires from people all over the country wanting parts or hardware for their Napanee cabinets. The company emphasizes that they no longer have parts for the old Napanee cabinets. However, they do welcome visitors to their showroom.

The old Coppes Brothers factory building in Nappanee is still in use. Modern Napanee built-in kitchen cabinets are now manufactured in the same building where the Napanee Dutch Kitchenets were built. The Coppes showroom on the left is open to the public.

No. 16 Oak.

Top of base 29x48 with zinc pan 17x33. Height 83 inches. Brass trimmed and castered. Wt. crated 280 pounds. **Finished**—Golden gloss. Weathered, Golden wax and Early English wax.   **$28.50**

No. 15 Oak.

Finished top 28x48. Height 80 inches. Brass trimmed and castered. Weight crated 270 pounds. **Finished**—Golden gloss, Weathered, Golden wax and Early English wax. Extra top for zinc top $1.25.
$27.00.

No. 3 Elm.

Base same as No. 1. Height 69 inches. Golden finish, brass trimmed and castered. Weight crated 160 pounds. Extra for zinc top $1.25.   **$19.30.**

No. 4 Elm.

Base same as No. 1. Height 85 inches. Golden finish, brass trimmed and castered. Weight crated 215 pounds. Extra for zinc top $1.25.   **$23.50.**

Coppes, Zook & Mutschler Co. Catalog (Circa 1905)

No. 1911 Elm.

Base same as No. 19. Height 75 inches. **Chipped glass** doors and 7x12 French plate in door to medicine cabinet. Golden finish, brass **trimmed** and castered. Weight crated 245 pounds. Extra for zinc top $1.25.
$26.00.

No. 16¼ Oak.

Top of base 29x48 with zinc pan 17x33. Height 88 inches. Brass trimmed and castered. Wt. crated 280 pounds. **Finished**—Golden gloss, Weathered, Golden wax and Early English wax.
$29.00.

No. 29 Elm.

Top 28x48. Height 85 inches. Golden finish. Weight crated 185 pounds. Extra for zinc top $1.25.
$19.00.

No. 17 Oak.

Top 32x48 with zinc pan 17x33. Height 80 inches. Brass trimmed and castered. Wt. crated 300 pounds. **Finished**—Golden gloss.
$28.00.

Coppes, Zook & Mutschler Co. Catalog (Circa 1905)

No. 711 Oak.

Finished top on base 27x42. Height 75 inches. Chipped glass doors and 7x12 French plate in door to medicine cabinet. Brass trimmed and castered. Weight crated 260 lbs. **Finished**—Golden gloss, Weathered, Golden wax or Early English wax. Extra for zinc top $1.25. **$24.50.**

No. 21 Elm.

Base same as No. 19. Height 76 inches. Golden finish, brass trimmed and castered. Weight crated 225 pounds. Extra for zinc top $1.25. **$23.30.**

No. 610 Elm.

Top 27x42. Height 74 inches. Chipped glass doors. Golden finish. Wt. crated 150 pounds. Extra for zinc top $1.25. **$16.00.**

No. 28 Elm.

Top 28x48. Height 68 inches. Golden finish. Weight crated 135 pounds. Extra for zinc top $1.25. **$14.80.**

Coppes, Zook & Mutschler Co. Catalog (Circa 1905)

The Dutch Kitchenet
Makes Kitchen Work Easier

BILL HOOKS

LOOK FOR DUTCH KITCHENET NAME PLATE

ROUND CORNERS AND EDGES EASY TO CLEAN

COOK BOOK HOLDER

EASY TO FILL & EASY TO CLEAN FLOUR BIN

WHITE ENAMELED CUPBOARDS

SIMPLE FLOUR SIFTER

DUST PROOF ROLL CURTAIN

SPICE JARS AND SALT DISH

TEA & COFFEE JARS

SUGAR SIFTER & LUMP CRUSHER

ALUMINUM OR PORCELAIN SLIDING TABLE TOP

VENTILATION OF CUPBOARD

KNEADING BOARD

CHOPPING BLOCK

PARTITIONED DRAWER

SLIDING WIRE SHELVES

SLIDING SHELF

RACK FOR PAN LIDS

CAKE & BREAD BOX

SLIDING BOTTOM SAVES STOOPING

HIGH ENOUGH TO SWEEP UNDER

Every Woman Should Read This FREE Book

It tells how to make kitchen work easy. Did you ever stop to think that a woman uses a larger number and a greater variety of tools in her kitchen than any man uses in his work? Then, too, she uses a great diversity of supplies and—she must clean her tools at least three times every day. Why not make the daily grind of tiresome housework as easy as possible? It is monotonous enough at best. The same old job of cooking—baking—dishwashing—over and over again—365 days every year.

The Dutch Kitchenet is more than an ordinary kitchen cabinet. It is handsomely finished and "Built Like Fine Furniture" by expert cabinet makers. Every detail is perfect and it has many exclusive new features that are very convenient.

The Woman's Work Bench

Look for NAPANEE DUTCH KITCHENET This Name Plate

This book explains fully the Dutch Kitchenet, a conveniently arranged—systemized—woman's work bench, that is more necessary to a woman than a desk or work bench to a man.

Send Coupon today for this Book, and address of the Dutch Kitchenet Dealer in your city who is authorized to guarantee every Dutch Kitchenet he sells.

Coppes Bros. & Zook   457 Market St.   Nappanee, Ind.

Mail Coupon For FREE Book

Coppes Bros. & Zook,
457 Market Street, Nappanee, Ind.

Please send me your Free Book "The Woman's Work Bench."

_____

_____

This restored 1916 Napanee Dutch Kitchenet is on display in the Coppes factory showroom. This old cabinet features a large flour bin that swings down to a horizontal position for filling. A large metal cap is then removed from the back of the flour bin to fill it. The two doors above the roll have etched glass panels. A metal bread box and sliding wire shelves are behind the long narrow door on the right side of cabinet base.

*The "Dutch Kitchenet" Systematizes Your Kitchen

It is a complete, sanitary kitchenet that has a place for everything you need in cooking or baking, conveniently arranged within easy reach, to give the greatest possible efficiency and save time, needless steps and work. It is equipped with many conveniences and little labor-saving devices not found in the old-fashioned kitchen cabinets.

Get a "Dutch Kitchenet" and make your kitchen work easy by using modern kitchen efficiency methods. Why be all fagged out and suffer from backache and headache? Why be a kitchen drudge, waste your strength and wear yourself out? A "Dutch Kitchenet" will systematize your kitchen work—make it easy and give you leisure time for rest and recreation.

The "Dutch Kitchenet" Makes Kitchen Work Easy !

The "Dutch Kitchenet" was designed by experts in kitchen efficiency and is a complete, fully equipped kitchenet with every modern convenience and labor-saving device. It is sanitary in every detail and has been approved by The Good Housekeeping Institute and Domestic Science experts. Read these 20 sanitary features carefully. Besides these sanitary features there are 20 other conveniences and labor-saving devices that save time and work.

1. Sanitary Base Construction.
2. Sanitary Snow-White Enamel Interior.
3. Sanitary Removable Flour Bin.
4. Sanitary Ventilated Bread and Cake Box.
5. Sanitary Ventilated Cooling Compartment.
6. Sanitary Bar Wire Shelves.
7. Sanitary Rounded Corners.
8. Sanitary Removable Sliding Table Top.
9. Sanitary Dust-Proof Roll Curtain.
10. Sanitary Sugar Jar.
11. Sanitary Sliding Bottom.
12. Sanitary Legs with Easy Working Castors.
13. Sanitary Dust-Proof Back.
14. Sanitary Velvet Finish.
15. Sanitary White Wood Kneading Board.
16. Sanitary Chopping Block.
17. Sanitary Meat Grinder Attachment.
18. Sanitary Coffee, Tea and Spice Jars.
19. Sanitary Yoke Hanger.
20. Sanitary White Enamel Cupboard.

TO DEALERS We want reliable dealers to represent us where there is no "Dutch Kitchenet" dealer. Write for exclusive agency proposition, terms, territory, etc. Our liberal proposition and sales co-operation plans will interest you.

Write now for this **FREE BOOK** and card of introduction to your local dealer. Only one dealer in each city sells the "Dutch Kitchenet". He is our exclusive representative and will be glad to show you the "Dutch Kitchenet" without any obligation on your part whatever. Just send a postcard with your address.

COPPES BROS.& ZOOK

447 Market St., Nappanee, Ind.

© _C. B. & Z. 9-20

The Indorsement of Success

COPPES BROTHERS & ZOOK
NAPPANEE, INDIANA

NAPANEE DUTCH KITCHENET

Napanee Dutch Kitchenets are good Merchandise

Pictorial Review September, 1920

How Many Steps
in the kitchen preparing three simple meals?

Mr. H. H. Tice, of the Emerson Engineers, noting the record of stop watch and pedometer on the preparation of a meal

A Statement by Mr. Harrington Emerson

It is very clear from our scientific studies of the preparation of meals with and without a Napanee Dutch Kitchenet, that its economies are along three entirely distinct lines:

1—Saving of effort, fatigue elimination.
2—Saving of time.
3—Standardization of work.

The saving of energy, shown by the large reduction in the number of steps, is very striking.

Harrington Emerson

FREE

The full story of all the tests made by the Emerson Engineers, told in a book, "Scientific Studies of Kitchen Work." This is an account of the most important tests ever made for women. They show how to end her greatest hardship—constant fatigue.

Mr. Emerson is a member of the Committee on Elimination of Waste in Industry, organized by Mr. Herbert Hoover.

The coupon brings you the book without charge.

2,113 steps every day—1,592 can be saved!

Harrington Emerson, "Father of Efficiency Engineers," finds by scientific measurement 2,113 steps taken in average kitchen every day. Proves 1,592 steps can be saved. Shows useless drudgery and terrible burden of fatigue housewives suffer. No one will now endure it longer.

AMAZING discoveries have resulted from Mr. Emerson's scientific time and motion studies on the preparation of meals. They are of vast importance.

Thousands of dollars were spent on these studies. Two famous domestic scientists were employed as counselors. Stop watches were used to record the time of preparing each meal and of each individual operation in preparing it. Pedometers, which measure distance walked, were used to register every step taken.

349 steps saved on this breakfast alone!

Fruit	Biscuits
Scrambled Eggs	Coffee

This simple breakfast was prepared in an average kitchen first without and then with a Napanee Dutch Kitchenet. Each operation in getting each meal was repeated by different operators to insure accuracy of result. It was found that in preparing and clearing away breakfast without a Napanee Kitchenet, 466 steps were taken.

That in preparing the same meal, by the same operators, in the same kitchen, with a Napanee only 117 steps were taken. 349 steps were saved! And the time was reduced 10 per cent. Good news for overworked women, this!

Supremely important results

By the same scientific procedure it was found that in preparing luncheon the steps saved by the Napanee actually totaled 509. And lunch was ready in 15 per cent less time. In preparing dinner 734 steps were saved! And 10 per cent of time!

In preparing the three meals without the Napanee 2,113 steps were taken, and only 521 in preparing with the Napanee.

Thus 1,592 steps were saved—three-fourths of the total—by the use of the Napanee. No woman need spend another exhausting day in the kitchen.

We ourselves were amazed

After these amazing discoveries no woman will end another day footsore and weary. None will endure the distressing fatigue of kitchen work any longer.

In simple justice to yourself learn all the relief you can get from the constant burden of kitchen work. The full story of Mr. Emerson's tests is told in a book, "Scientific Studies of Kitchen Work." Send the coupon for it today.

Go also to your dealer. Let him show you the use of the Napanee. See for yourself the more scientific design, the superior construction, the greater conveniences that give the Napanee its amazing value to you.

What Stop Watch and Pedometer Showed

PREPARING	No. Steps Without Napanee	No. Steps With Napanee	No. Steps Saved	Time Saved
Breakfast . . .	466	117	349	10%
Lunch	651	142	509	15%
Dinner	996	262	734	10%
Hot Biscuits .	176	25	151	13%
Roasting Meat	160	30	130	16%
Combination Salad . . .	100	66	34	9%
French Dressing	80	5	75	50%
Apple Pie . . .	260	36	224	10%
Coffee	100	15	85	41.5%
Making Bread	330	18	312	7%

Napanee Dutch Kitchenet

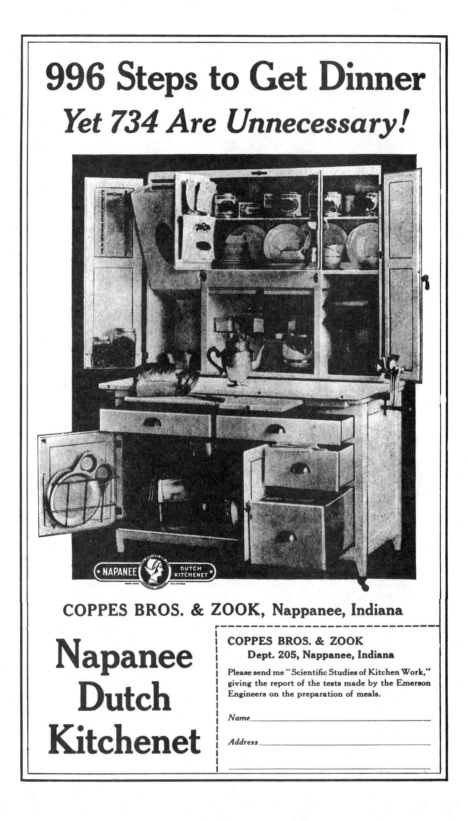

996 Steps to Get Dinner
Yet 734 Are Unnecessary!

COPPES BROS. & ZOOK, Nappanee, Indiana

Napanee Dutch Kitchenet

COPPES BROS. & ZOOK
Dept. 205, Nappanee, Indiana

Please send me "Scientific Studies of Kitchen Work," giving the report of the tests made by the Emerson Engineers on the preparation of meals.

Name_____

Address_____

Restored Napanee Dutch Kitchenet cabinet. Circa 1927. This cabinet is made from mixed woods and was originally painted. Note the small flour bin that pulls out for filling. The swing out sugar jar is mounted on the left beneath the flour bin.

5

McDougall Cabinets

The McDougall company began when George P. McDougall, a civil war veteran, started building kitchen tables and pie safes in the rear of a storeroom in Indianapolis. The business was small but successful. After finishing high school, his son, Charles P. McDougall, entered his father's business to learn the furniture making trade. About 1895 George McDougall built a new plant on South Meridian Street in Indianapolis to manufacture kitchen furniture. In 1898 the name of the company was changed to G.P. McDougall & Son.

Charles McDougall quickly learned the operation of the kitchen furniture plant. With a desire to know more about the furniture business, young McDougall persuaded his father to let him go West. While in California he noticed that, instead of building ordinary kitchen tables such as produced in his father's plant, some manufacturers were adding pull-out flour bins. Returning to Indianapolis, Charles McDougall convinced his father to equip their tables with flour bins. Later, Charles McDougall added cabinet tops to the kitchen tables. These early kitchen cabinets are known today as baker's cabinets or "possum belly" cabinets. Similar tables and cabinets were made around the turn of the century by other Indiana kitchen cabinet manufacturers.

George McDougall died in 1901 and Charles McDougall took control of his father's business. After organizing the business so that it would continue to operate in his absence, the younger McDougall traveled to Germany and Holland to study German and Dutch kitchens. As shown by the 1905 McDougall cabinets on the following pages, the European influence was evident in the McDougall cabinets built for the next few years. These early McDougall cabinets are rare today and the command relatively high prices.

On September 22, 1909 the McDougall plant in Indianapolis and eight adjoining homes were destroyed by a disastrous fire started by as disgruntled watchman who wanted a vacation. The loss was in excess of $120,000, a large amount of money in 1909. Undaunted by the setback, Charles McDougall decided to purchase the former Hoke Manufacturing plant in Frankfort, Indiana about 30 miles northwest of Indianapolis. Three or four Frankfort businessmen joined McDougall as investors and officers of the new McDougall

Company. McDougall and his partners equipped the former Hoke plant with the latest woodworking machinery and equipment available. When the McDougall Company started back in operation in 1910, the new factory in Frankfort was one of the most modern furniture plants in the country at that time.

The 60,000 square foot plant at Frankfort included a huge drying kiln for the lumber used in the cabinets, a mechanical room where the thoroughly seasoned lumber was cut to size and shaped, an assembly room, and several offices. A basement under the large machine room housed the veneering department and the tool room. The motors for the various woodworking tools in the machine room were also housed in the basement. The sawdust from the various machines was collected by a suction system and sent to the heating plant where it was burned as fuel.

The McDougall cabinets built at Frankfort were quite different from the earlier cabinets built at Indianapolis. They more closely resembled the cabinets offered by other kitchen cabinet manufacturers. However, the was one notable difference in the McDougall cabinet. The patented *Auto-Front* roll door dropped down to open rather than roll up as on most cabinets. In the open position the door was stored in a compartment below the lower shelf of the top section. In the closed position the door was held in place by a special latch. This latch is usually missing or broken on most McDougall cabinets found today. Unfortunately, there is not a replacement available for the McDougall Auto-Front latch at this time.

The porcelain work tops for the McDougall cabinets were made by the Ingram-Richardson Manufacturing Company, also located in Frankfort. Ingram-Richardson was probably the largest manufacturer of porcelain cabinet tops and table tops. They provided porcelain tops for many of the other major manufacturers of kitchen cabinets.

The large McDougall flour bin swung out from the top for easy filling. It could also be easily removed for cleaning. The flour bins in the 1911 McDougall cabinets had full glass fronts that revealed the contents at a glance. The crystal-glass sugar jar had a dispenser that allowed sugar to flow freely when required. A rack mounted between the flour bin and the sugar jar held crystal-glass jars for coffee, tea, and spices. Until about 1920 the drawers had stamped metal pulls which were later replaced by cast handles. The bottom cupboard had a lower sliding shelf that provided easy access to large utensils and a sliding wire shelf for smaller pots and pans.

Most McDougall cabinets manufactured prior to the early 1920s were natural finished oak. The interiors of the cabinets made after 1910 were enameled white. Oak was used primarily for the exterior construction of the McDougall cabinets. In 1913 the company used 300,000 board feet of oak alone each month. Other woods used for the interior construction included elm, cottonwood, and gum. In 1920 all of the cabinets in the McDougall line were available with a natural oak or white enamel finish.

By the late 1920s the famous McDougall Auto-Front roll door had been replaced by a conventional roll-up door. The smaller flour bins on later McDougall cabinets were mounted on arms that allowed them to be pulled forward and down for filling. This flour bin was manufactured by McCormick Brothers of Albany, Indiana and was also used in Sellers cabinets. Most of the McDougall cabinets built in the late 1920s and early 1930s were probably finished in white enamel or other colors.

The McDougall Company was adversely affected by the depression and in late November, 1931 the company filed for reorganization. Charles McDougall was no longer involved in the day-to-day operation of the company, but he was still a member of the board. Although McDougall never married and apparently had few close friends, he was a well-liked and respected member of the Frankfort business community. On the morning of November 24, 1933 Charles McDougall drove his new car to a farm north of Frankfort. He tied one end of a long rope around his waist and the other end to a large block of cork. He then plunged off a steep cliff into the cold water of a gravel pit located on the farm. Within a year or two after his death, the McDougall Company was defunct.

McDougall cabinet. Circa 1898. This unusually short cabinet was one of the first McDougall kitchen cabinets. It shows how the McDougall cabinet evolved from the kitchen table by adding the upper section and the swing down bins below. Note the small drawers and doors in the sparse upper section.

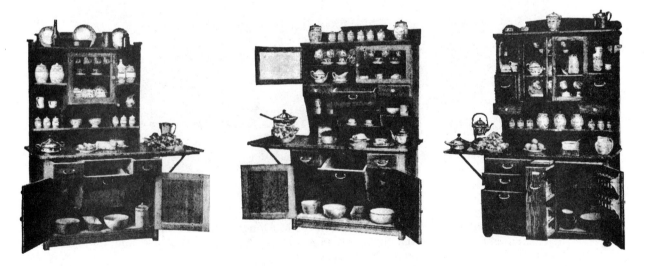

G. P. McDougall & Son

502 Terminal Building   INDIANAPOLIS, IND.

From *The Ladies Home Journal* October, 1905

McDougall Kitchen Cabinets

are designed expressly for the convenience of the woman who does kitchen work.
Every article needed in cooking, baking, or the preparation of any meal, including the food supplies, can be kept in a McDougall Kitchen Cabinet, where it is within instant reach of the hand without the taking of a single step. You can get one

On 30 Days' Trial In Your Own Home

where you can use the cabinet and see for yourself how many steps and how much extra work it will save you every day, and how it will help you economize on food supplies.

The Ideal Christmas Gift for Wife or Mother

Write today for our handsomely illustrated catalogue, showing the different styles, that will enable you to quickly ascertain the particular cabinet your wife or mother would like to have, ranging in price from $15.75 to $54.00, that you can order it for Christmas from your dealer without her knowledge.

Look for the name-plate, "*McDougall, Indianapolis.*" It is the maker's guaranty for quality—your protection against imitation.

G. P. McDougall & Son, 528 Terminal Bldg., Indianapolis, Ind.

McDougall cabinet. Circa 1905. This rare old McDougall cabinet was built at the Indianapolis factory. Note the numerous drawers in the upper section of this beautiful oak cabinet. The three swing down bins in the upper section were probably used for sugar, coffee, and other bulk staples. The large bin on the right side of the cabinet base was used for potatoes or other vegetables. The device mounted on the right side of the work top is a cherry pitter.

McDougall

Auto-Front Half Open
Front disappears as shown in large picture

Auto-Front Closed
Perfect protection from dust and dirt

The New Auto-Front McDougall
Patented and Trade-Mark Registered

 I WILL make each kitchen hour a joy — each meal a source of keenest pleasure — each day an example of economy and efficiency. I radiate good cheer.

I will banish blue Monday and black Friday — take the drudgery out of your kitchen — and fill the days with the song of willing service.

I will keep your kitchen as neat as wax — your food supplies in perfect order. I will save you all I cost in a score of ways — to live without me is an extravagance.

I will always be on time — morning, noon and night — always keep my temper — never aggravate — never disappoint you — for I am the McDougall Kitchen Cabinet.

I will give you the manifold benefits of the latest improvement in kitchen service — the McDougall Auto-Front — that vanishes at the touch of the finger, and is the *open sesame* to culinary delights.

I will come to you any day and stay for years — upon payment of only $1.00 a week (for a short time). Come and see me at your local furniture store.

I will send you "My Book" for the asking. It describes styles and quotes prices. Write for it today.

Your faithful servant,

Patience McDougall

McDougall Co., Frankfort, Ind., U. S. A.

The Saturday Evening Post August 26, 1916

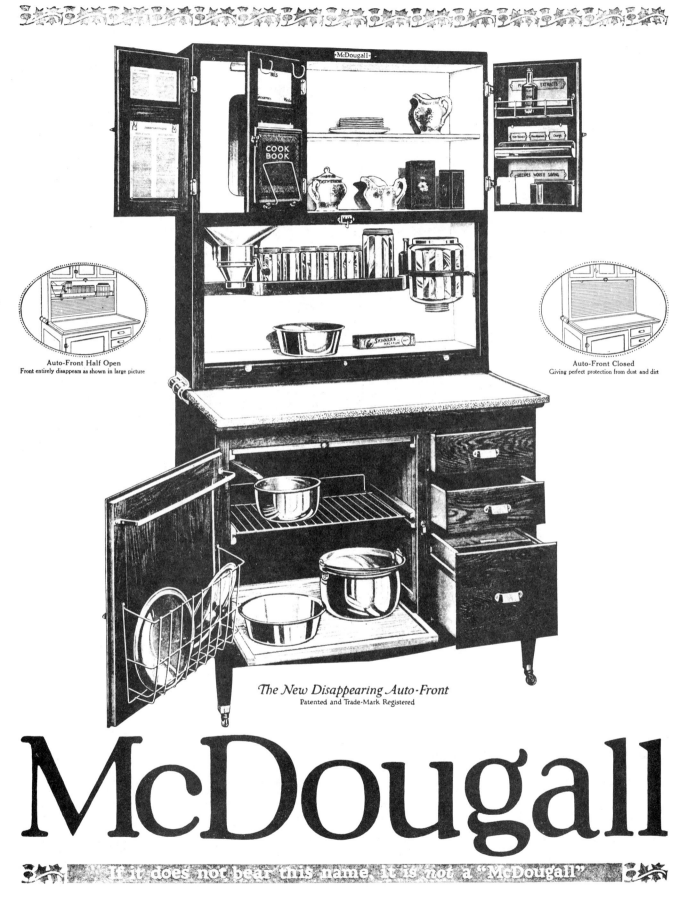

Auto-Front Half Open
Front entirely disappears as shown in large picture

Auto-Front Closed
Giving perfect protection from dust and dirt

The New Disappearing Auto-Front
Patented and Trade-Mark Registered

McDougall

If it does not bear this name, it is not a "McDougall"

The Saturday Evening Post September 16, 1916

All the Latest Improvements
are in the McDougall

The McDougall has the new, snow-white porceliron extension tabletop—that never requires scrubbing or scouring—that is as sanitary as glass, but will not chip or break—that nothing can stain or mar.

—has the new leg base—that you can sweep under without moving the cabinet—a sanitary feature of the greatest importance.

—has the new, easy filling, removable, open-faced flour bin, with attached magic sifter—that supplies the exact amount of flour needed.

—has durable, pure white enamelled cupboards and compartments—to hold a full supply of package goods and necessary china.

—has large, swinging, crystal-glass, metal-top sugar bin, with new quick-action shutter, from which the sugar flows freely as required.

—has crystal-glass, metal-top jars, plainly marked for coffee, tea, spices—with sifter-tops for salt and pepper.

—has racks for cook-books, extracts, tickets, small change—bill spindles—reference tables—order reminder—meat board and chopper stand.

—has roomy drawers or knives, forks, spoons and all small articles—for linens and towels—all neatly and conveniently divided.

—has large cupboard with sliding bottom and sliding shelf, containing ample room for all kettles, pots, pans and other large utensils.

—has big, all-metal bread and cake drawer, with automatic cover and sliding shelf—that keeps bread and pastry fresh and sweet.

—has lacquered artcraft trimmings, ball-bearing casters, art-panel doors—and all the latest improvements in kitchen efficiency.

—has graceful lines—superfine cabinet work, and is daintily finished with steam-proof varnish that retains its lustre indefinitely.

In addition to all these advantages, the McDougall is the only kitchen cabinet made that has the patented Auto-Front feature—which adds immensely to its beauty and convenience.

The McDougall Auto-Front is therefore the one perfect Kitchen Cabinet—the undisputed "Steinway of the kitchen."

"Won't Daddy be surprised that I've made my own birthday cake, mother?"
"Yes, dear, and I'm proud you did, with only the McDougall to help you."

ARE you fitting your daughter by example and experience to be a successful home-maker?

Are you encouraging her to take keen delight in cooking and baking? Are you educating her for the practical work of life? Are you teaching her true economy and efficiency?

Economy comes from knowing how to get the best results for the least expenditure—efficiency comes from accomplishment with the least effort. Each is an essential factor.

In kitchen work, both economy and efficiency find their real development in the McDougall with the Auto-Front feature—securing the best results from the least expenditure—in time, labor, money—all with the least possible effort.

The Auto-Front device (patented and trade-mark registered) consists of a flexible wooden curtain that drops and raises at the finger's touch—leaves no slot or groove to catch dirt and foods—adds over one-third more working surface—does away forever with doors which obstruct the table top.

The McDougall Auto-Front makes kitchen work easier, simpler, quicker—and more interesting.

The McDougall Auto-Front cuts the time spent in the kitchen practically in half—gives you leisure for other things—thus adds to the joy of living—all for only $1.00 a week, for a short time.

You cannot spend this small amount in any way that will be of greater daily benefit to your daughter, your family and yourself.

Visit your McDougall dealer today—let him demonstrate the advantages of the McDougall Auto-Front. Then, have him send you one on approval—so you can test it in practical use.

Also, write—now—for description, prices and dealer's name to McDougall Company, Frankfort, Ind.

McDougall

The Auto-Front feature can be had only on cabinets bearing this name

The Saturday Evening Post March 2, 1917

The Furnishing of the Modern Kitchen begins with the

McDougall

Go to your furniture store and see the McDougall Kitchen Cabinet with the patented Auto-Front—the device that does away with swinging doors over the table-top and adds one-third more working surface. No other cabinet has this exclusive McDougall feature—so be sure you see the McDougall—look for the name "McDougall" on the front of the cabinet, above the upper cupboard.

Compare the McDougall (if you wish) with any other cabinet—and see for yourself how it excels all others in design, in conveniences, in finish—in beauty, in efficiency, in service.

See These Exclusive Features

The Auto-Front—that drops and raises at the finger's touch, instantly closing the work-cupboard, and leaving no slot or groove to catch dirt or foods.

The quick-filling Flour Bin with magic sifter—that enables you to measure the exact amount of sifted flour you need.

The all-metal Bread and Cake Drawer, with automatic cover—that keeps bread and pastry fresh and sweet.

The extra large Utensil Cupboard with sliding base and sliding shelf—that holds all large kitchen utensils, with room to spare.

The swinging, crystal-glass Sugar Jar with automatic shutter—that shows at a glance exactly how much sugar you have on hand.

Make These Practical Tests

Pull out the snow-white Porceliron Extension Table Top—to prove how large a working surface it gives you, even with the Auto-Front closed. Note how you can prepare the most delicate foods on it—because it is so sanitary.

Take a broom and sweep under the Sanitary Leg Base—to prove that you need not move the McDougall to keep your floor neat and clean.

Stand in front of the McDougall and see how easily and quickly you can put your hand on anything it contains—to prove how much time it will save you every day.

Pull out the Drawers and push them in again—to prove how easily they work, and that they never bind or stick. Note how well they are finished, inside and out.

Have It Sent on Approval

You need not buy the McDougall until you have first had an opportunity to try it in daily use in your own home, and know from actual experience that it is the most useful article you ever had.

Your furniture dealer will deliver it without cost. After you have satisfied yourself that it is the Steinway of the Kitchen—the only Kitchen Cabinet that meets every possible need—then pay as little as $1.00 a week for it. It will save many times this amount for years.

Don't wait another day. Visit your dealer now—today—and get this "automatic maid" to help you in a hundred ways to make kitchen work easier, kitchen hours shorter, kitchen time the most joyous time of all the day.

If your local dealer does not have the McDougall Auto-Front, write for illustrated booklet showing various styles and sizes in McDougall Kitchen Cabinets at prices from $14.50 to $54.00—and we will arrange for you to get one. If you are going to build, instruct your architect to plan a space for a movable, sanitary-base McDougall in your kitchen. We will gladly send him details.

Made only by McDougall Company, Frankfort, Ind., U. S. A.

McDOUGALL

McDougall

"The Steinway of the Kitchen"

The Auto-Front feature—patented and trade-mark registered—can be had only in the McDougall. It consists of a flexible curtain, that extends the full width of the Cabinet, drops or raises at the finger's touch, but leaves no slot or groove to catch dirt or foods. It adds one-third more working surface, while doing away entirely with swinging doors which obstruct the table-top. The McDougall leads in improvements, and excels in every efficiency test.

Have the McDougall Sent Home on Approval

You can make *no* mistake in buying the McDougall—especially after you have *used* it in your own kitchen, have *proved* how much time and work it saves, have *demonstrated* how completely it excels in design, in construction, in service, in economy and in improvements.

Your furniture dealer will *deliver* any McDougall Kitchen Cabinet *you select*—prices $14.50 to $54.00, varying with design—to *your own home*. After you have *satisfied* yourself that *you need the McDougall*, you can pay for it at the rate of $1.00 a week.

Write McDougall Company, Frankfort, Indiana, U. S. A., for Illustrated Catalog.

Before you build or remodel your home, write to McDougall Company for free plans of Model Efficiency Kitchens

McDougall oak cabinet. Circa 1917. This restored McDougall cabinet features slag glass panels in the upper doors. The Auto-Front roll door spans the full width of the cabinet. The large flour bin and sifter is partially hidden by the left upper door. The crystal-glass sugar jar is mounted in a swing out bracket on the right side of the cabinet. All of the hardware is original.

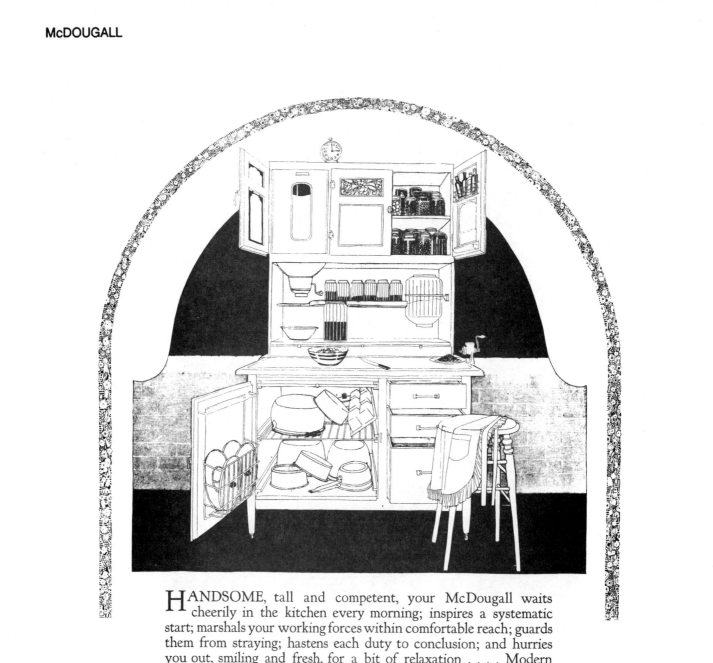

HANDSOME, tall and competent, your McDougall waits cheerily in the kitchen every morning; inspires a systematic start; marshals your working forces within comfortable reach; guards them from straying; hastens each duty to conclusion; and hurries you out, smiling and fresh, for a bit of relaxation . . . . Modern descendant of the first kitchen cabinet is your McDougall. Ancestral leadership, steadfastly upheld, exhibits itself in fine character of construction and complete convenience . . . . Lustrous beauty, sound oak sturdiness and rare utility combined—brightener of kitchen appearance, lightener of dreary routine—your McDougall.

Exclusively McDougall: Auto-Front, the famous patented wood curtain which drops open automatically; the immaculate table top which is rigid when extended; the mortised and tenoned joints throughout; the steel braced sanitary base; the finish of enduring luster; and numerous exclusive refinements. Visit the McDougall dealer's display or write for "The McDougall Method," a book that describes helpful kitchen arrangement and the eight McDougalls in white or oak.

MCDOUGALL COMPANY, FRANKFORT, INDIANA, U. S. A.

McDougall
THE FIRST KITCHEN CABINET

McDougall cabinet. Circa 1920. This beautifully restored 48-inch wide oak cabinet is in mint condition. The large flour bin is hidden by the long door on the left. The Auto-Front roll door in the center of the upper section closes to hide the sugar jar, coffee jar, and the spice jars. All of the bright nickel-plated hardware is original.

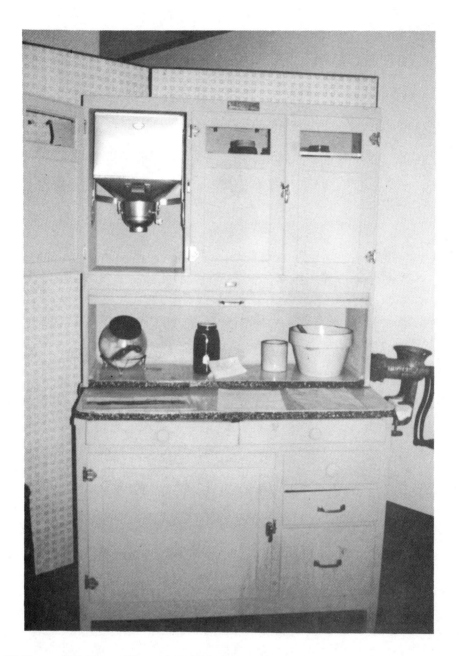

McDougall cabinet. Circa 1927. This restored painted cabinet is displayed at the Clinton County Historical Society in Frankfort, Indiana. This cabinet features a full-width conventional roll door that replaced the famous McDougall Auto-Front roll door. The flour bin mounted on a special bracket that allows it to be pulled forward and down for filling. The bottom shelf of the upper section is porcelain to match the sliding work top. The sugar jar sets in a wire rack on the bottom shelf. Three of the drawer handles have been replaced by wood knobs.

6

Boone Cabinets

The Boone kitchen cabinets were manufactured by the Campbell-Smith-Ritchie Company in Lebanon, Indiana about 25 miles northwest of Indianapolis. Campbell-Smith-Ritchie began as Campbell & Smith in 1892 when George Campbell and James Smith purchased the Lebanon Planing Mill, which was established just after the Civil War. In 1900 Morris Ritchie, who had been a grocer in Lebanon for about 20 years, sold his grocery store and became partner in the firm which then became Campbell-Smith-Ritchie.

Until the early 1900s Campbell-Smith-Ritchie was primarily a planing mill and lumberyard. They specialized in millwork such as making window and door frames, and decorative trim which was used extensively on homes at that time. They also sold building materials including lumber, cement, shingles, and lath.

We believe the company started making kitchen cabinets sometime about the turn of the century. Since the building trade was seasonal, they probably made kitchen cabinets and similar furniture to keep their workers busy during the winter months. In addition to kitchen cabinets, we believe that they also made cupboards and wardrobes.

On Sunday morning August 27, 1905, the Campbell-Smith-Ritchie planing mill and lumberyard was completely destroyed by a fire. Shortly after the fire, the company bought a parcel of land on the west edge of town and began the construction of the first building of what was to becomes a sprawling manufacturing complex.

The company's manufacturing operations flourished in their new quarters and in 1910 Campbell-Smith-Ritchie discontinued the lumberyard business to devote its full resources to manufacturing the kitchen cabinets which were rapidly growing in popularity. Lebanon is the county seat of Boone County and the company adopted the "Boone" name for its line of kitchen cabinets. Within a short time Campbell-Smith-Ritchie was booming as Lebanon's largest industry and its Boone kitchen cabinets were advertised and sold nationwide.

In 1922 the company announced three new models of Boone cabinets which they claimed were designed by 369 women from all over the United States. A full-page color ad in the August, 1922, issue of the *Ladies' Home Journal* displayed these new cabinets: the Mary Boone, the Dorothy Boone, and the Helen Boone. By 1925, four new models had been added to the Boone line of kitchen cabinets. These new models included the Bertha Boone, the Betty Boone, the Boone No.47, and the Boone No.79.

This new line of Boone cabinets boasted features and innovations that made the Boone cabinets one of the most unique kitchen cabinets at that time. Standard features for the Mary Boone, Helen Boone, and Bertha Boone included: a disappearing ironing board, a built-in alarm clock, a mirror, an electric light at the top of the cabinet, and a desk section. Optional features included a coffee grinder which mounted to the side of the cabinet and a swing-out stool. The larger Bertha Boone, which featured a utility closet at each end, was designed so it could be built into the wall if desired. The smaller Betty Boone, which was only about 28 inches wide, was intended primarily for apartments and small homes. The Dorothy Boone was a low cabinet without a top unit. Only 35 inches high, it was designed to be place beneath the kitchen window.

The Boone No.47 and Boone No.79 were "stripped-down" versions of the Helen Boone and Mary Boone cabinets. They did not include the disappearing ironing board, alarm clock, mirror, desk section, electric light or other exclusive features of the Helen Boone and Mary Boone. The cabinets described above were advertised in leading magazines and were sold throughout the nation. Before the Campbell-Smith-Ritchie Company began advertising nationally, their cabinets were sold primarily in Indiana and adjoining midwestern states. Because we have been unable to find any Boone advertisements prior to 1922, it is somewhat difficult to identify and date these earlier Boone cabinets.

We have been able to identify some Boone cabinets built between 1910 and 1922 by their hardware and construction which are similar to the later Boone cabinets. However, these early Boone cabinets are rather simple and do not include many of the features found on later Boone models. The cabinets produced by Campbell-Smith-Ritchie after their planing mill burned in 1905 were probably quite different from cabinets built prior to the fire. Since most of the early patterns, hardware, and other equipment were destroyed by the fire, it is likely that they redesigned their cabinets to adapt to the new manufacturing facility built after the fire.

Like most other cabinet manufacturers, Campbell-Smith-Ritchie continued to prosper until the great depression of the 1930s. In its peak years of the 1920s the company had as many as 150 employees who worked five and a half days a week. However, throughout much of the 1930s the company operated on a three-days-a-week schedule. After the demand for free-standing cabinets declined in the early 1930s, the company began manufacturing built-in kitchen cabinets and oak breakfast sets. They also continued to build a few free-standing cabinets, although their construction more closely resembled the modern built-in cabinets. These later Boone cabinets had plain doors and lacked most of the special features of the Boone cabinets introduced in 1922.

Campbell-Smith-Ritchie was sold to an Indianapolis businessman in 1940. The business did not prove successful for the new owner. After operating at a loss for 18 months, the company went into receivership and the company that was once Lebanon's largest employer was history.

Campbell-Smith-Ritchie Company manufacturing facilities in Lebanon, Indiana about 1912. The long low buildings behind the factory buildings were probably used for the lumber and building materials business which the company discontinued in 1910. The large stacks of lumber shown in the center background were used for the production of kitchen cabinets. The two main factory buildings on the right still remain and are currently used by a plastics manufacturing company.

Boone cabinet. Circa 1912. This oak cabinet is one of the earliest Boone cabinets that we have seen. It featured a large swing out flour bin and etched glass in the upper doors. This cabinet is similar to early Napanee cabinets. The large bins in the base section are hidden by doors and were probably used for potatoes and other vegetables.

Helen Boone is as capable as she is fair to look upon

"Handsome *is* as Handsome *does*", runs the copybook maxim of happy memory. And it is still *true*. Boone Cabinets as represented by "Helen", below, *are* beautiful. But they are also unique in work-saving *service*. They are *capable* because they incorporate the proved, ultra-modern advantages 369 Women, readers of The Ladies' Home Journal, designed. See, compare; here, or at your Dealer's. No other cabinet has all of the Boone features. Send for our "Work-Saving" Booklet. Simply address:

CAMPBELL·SMITH·RITCHIE COMPANY
The Oldest Manufacturers of Kitchen Cabinets in America

Lebanon   Indiana

One Year Ago

a small advertisement appeared in this magazine, admitting that our kitchen cabinet was no better than the others and asking you women for practical suggestions.

~and Today

three marvelous kitchen cabinets, conceived from the ideas suggested by 369 women, stand out from all other cabinets—Mary, Helen, and Dorothy Boone.

Illustration shows Mary Boone Kitchen Cabinet

369 Women Designed these Three Boone Kitchen Cabinets

These features are worth much more to you than their slight additional cost.

You want a kitchen cabinet to save you time and work. The special women-designed features of Mary, Helen, and Dorothy Boone make them the most *economical* kitchen cabinets because they save you *so much more* time and work.

If your dealer does not yet show Helen, Mary, and Dorothy Boone Cabinets, please send us his name. Then we will send you a booklet of information and see that you can be conveniently served.

"WHICH kitchen cabinet shall I buy?" Could you have answered definitely a year ago? Even we, their oldest manufacturers, were forced to admit that we couldn't.

In one short year—what a change! Today three marvelous kitchen cabinets stand out, acclaimed, *preferred*—Mary Boone, Helen Boone, and Dorothy Boone—a triple tribute to the ingenuity of American women.

Last April we gave you women readers of The Ladies' Home Journal your first opportunity to say what *you* wanted in *your* kitchen cabinet. In the avalanche of enthusiastic replies were 369 letters suggesting practical, needed improvements of which mere man had never dreamed. No wonder Mary, Helen, and Dorothy Boone, created from these women-made suggestions,

have become famous in such a short space of time.

It is gratifying to find also that we are rapidly becoming the clearing house for practical ideas for further improving kitchen cabinets. Women are constantly sending us suggestions, many of them of great value to womankind. Boone kitchen cabinets will ever continue to be the most progressive, modern cabinets.

No longer need you accept kitchen cabinets limited in their utility by men's ideas. No longer need you question "which shall I buy?" On the first anniversary of Mary, Helen, and Dorothy Boone (the kitchen cabinets designed by 369 women), the tribute they are receiving from women everywhere points the sure way for your decision. Enjoy a Boone kitchen cabinet in your kitchen, too.

Only Boone Cabinets Have These Features

Built-in desk section. Your kitchen office. Compartments for cook books, expense books and recipe books; drawer for tickets, bills, keys and small change.
Built-in alarm clock. Recalls you to the kitchen when the bread is baked or the roast is done.
Plate glass mirror. For a hasty glance when the door bell rings.
Two electrical sockets. One for the electric iron, toaster, or heater, and one for light.

Disappearing ironing board. *Where* you want it *when* you want it. One push and it's out of your way.
Nested Drawers, with sliding extension table top.
Swinging Stool. Why stand on your feet all day? Work without weariness.
Sanitary "Katchall" for refuse. Detachable and convenient.
Arcade Crystal Coffee Mill, so you can grind your coffee fresh for every meal.

CAMPBELL-SMITH-RITCHIE CO., Lebanon, Ind.
The Oldest Manufacturers of Kitchen Cabinets in America

Boone KITCHEN CABINETS

The Ladies Home Journal April, 1923

Oak Boone cabinet. Circa 1924. This Helen Boone cabinet has been stripped of many of its original features such as the flour bin, the clock, and the desk section. However, the built-in hidden ironing board is still intact and is shown in position for use. All of the hardware is original.

"Month of May Exposition"
of Boone
DESIGNED BY 369 WOMEN

to acquaint all women with *Boone* exclusive conveniences

Co-operating with "Better Homes Week" May 10 to 17, announced by Secretary Herbert Hoover and endorsed by the club women of most states.

AGAIN *Boone* is first to consider the interests of the woman in the home, and first to meet her needs.

Just as men find it essential, in the efficient operation of business, to attend expositions of business equipment—women now find it essential to the more easy and pleasant performance of their household duties, to keep informed regarding the latest improvements in household equipment.

A "Month of May" *Boone* Exposition is therefore being held to give you personally an opportunity to see for yourself how much more enjoyable a *Boone* will make your kitchen duties—to really appreciate how fully the numerous exclusive *Boone* features, *designed by 369 women*, provide for your every need—and to decide which of the seven new *Boone* models best suits you.

Moreover, this Exposition is held in your own city, from May 1st to May 30th, at the store of a leading furniture dealer, so you can easily attend it. These progressive merchants are showing special exhibits of unusual interest during the entire month of May.

Whether you contemplate the addition of a *Boone* to your present kitchen facilities or not, here is an ideal opportunity to see for yourself the extraordinary comfort and convenience of a *Boone*, *designed by 369 women.*

CAMPBELL-SMITH-RITCHIE COMPANY
The Oldest Manufacturers of Kitchen Cabinets in America
LEBANON · INDIANA

Child's Play Cabinet free at your dealer's

Your local furniture dealer will give you a cardboard cut-out of a miniature *Mary Boone* which children cherish for their doll houses.

This is a Boone Year

Mary Boone, *designed by 369 women*
Fully equipped and with these exclusive features: disappearing ironing board, electric light, extra appliance socket, desk section, card index for recipes, mirror, alarm clock to time cooking, daily reminder, coffee mill. Finest construction. White or gray enamel.

Betty Boone *designed by 369 women*

A completely equipped cabinet for kitchenette apartments and small homes. Only 2 ft. 3½ in. wide. Several exclusive Boone features.

Bertha Boone *designed by 369 women*
Can be built into the wall if desired. A large, permanent, extra utility closet at each end. Has all the exclusive *Boone* features of *Mary Boone.*

Helen Boone *designed by 369 women*
Has the same exclusive features as *Mary Boone.* The two cutlery drawers and bread board slide out with table top, giving accessibility.

at your local furniture store

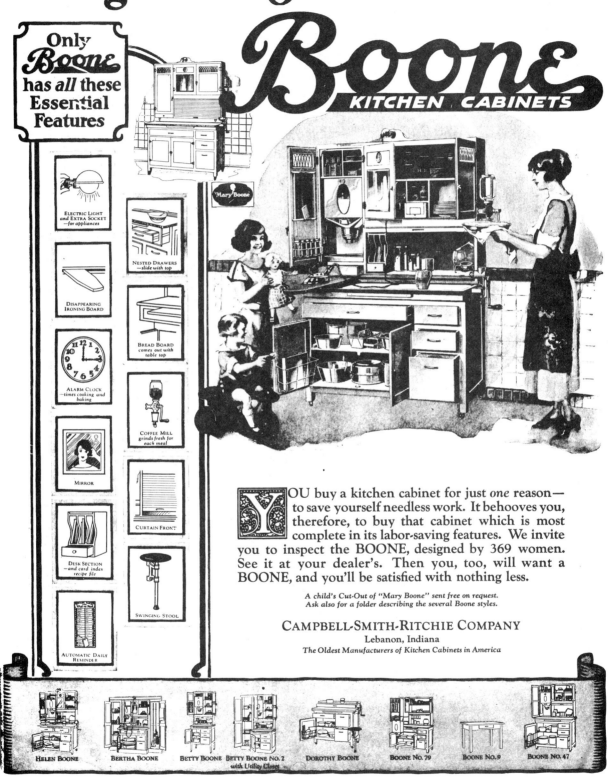

Designed by 369 Women

Boone KITCHEN CABINETS

Only Boone has all these Essential Features

- ELECTRIC LIGHT and EXTRA SOCKET —for appliances
- DISAPPEARING IRONING BOARD
- ALARM CLOCK —times cooking and baking
- MIRROR
- DESK SECTION —and card index recipe file
- AUTOMATIC DAILY REMINDER
- NESTED DRAWERS —slide with top
- BREAD BOARD comes out with table top
- COFFEE MILL grinds fresh for each meal
- CURTAIN FRONT
- SWINGING STOOL

YOU buy a kitchen cabinet for just *one* reason— to save yourself needless work. It behooves you, therefore, to buy that cabinet which is most complete in its labor-saving features. We invite you to inspect the BOONE, designed by 369 women. See it at your dealer's. Then you, too, will want a BOONE, and you'll be satisfied with nothing less.

A child's Cut-Out of "Mary Boone" sent free on request.
Ask also for a folder describing the several Boone styles.

CAMPBELL-SMITH-RITCHIE COMPANY
Lebanon, Indiana
The Oldest Manufacturers of Kitchen Cabinets in America

HELEN BOONE · BERTHA BOONE · BETTY BOONE · BETTY BOONE No. 2 with Utility Closet · DOROTHY BOONE · BOONE No. 79 · BOONE No. 9 · BOONE No. 47

The Saturday Evening Post February 21, 1925

Helen Boone kitchen cabinet. Circa 1927. This Boone cabinet was restored by Mrs. Ruth Watson of Mooresville, Indiana. The cabinet was originally owned by Mrs. Watson's late parents, Mr. and Mrs. Archie Darnell of Monrovia, Indiana. One unique feature of this cabinet is a built-in ironing board which is concealed in a compartment just above the porcelain work top.

Boone cabinet. Circa 1929. This narrow cabinet was made for apartments and small homes. The flour bin mounted on the upper left door which pulled out at the top for filling. This Boone cabinet was originally painted.

Boone cabinet. Circa 1935. This Boone cabinet has flush paneled doors like the built-in cabinet produced by the company in the 1930s. The mixed woods used in the construction of this cabinet indicate that it was originally painted as were most cabinets produced at that time. The door latches are not original.

7

Other Cabinets

So far, we have introduced you to five of the largest manufacturers of "Hoosier" style kitchen cabinets. Of course, there were many other companies who made these cabinets. Between 1899 and 1949 there were more than 40 known manufacturers of the kitchen cabinets we know as "Hoosiers." The 1911 *Grand Rapids Furniture Record* listed eight manufacturers of kitchen cabinets, five of which were located in Indiana. In 1925 the same publication listed ten manufacturers with eight of them in Indiana.

Many of the early kitchen cabinet manufacturers were very small and have long been forgotten. However, other manufacturers produced a sizable number of cabinets and many of these "Hoosier" cabinets are still around. Some of the cabinets found today include: Wilson, Greencastle, Ariel, Kitchen Maid, Ideal, Shelby, Marsh, Tippecanoe, Vincennes, and others. In the mid-1920s Wilson was listed as the third largest manufacturer of kitchen cabinets; Hoosier was first and Sellers was second.

Wilson was one of the few major manufacturers of "Hoosier" cabinets that was not located in Indiana. The Wilson was made in Grand Rapids, Michigan which for many years was a leading furniture manufacturing center. Although we have been collecting kitchen cabinet advertisements for several years, we have never found any Wilson ads. The Wilson was sold by Sears Roebuck and Co. for many years and this may account for the lack of direct advertising by Wilson. Wilson cabinets are still rather plentiful and we have included photographs of some Wilson cabinets in this section.

The other cabinets shown in this section were made by some of the lesser known kitchen cabinet manufacturers. The manufacturer is unknown for a few the cabinets shown here. The first cabinet shown in this section is an unusual cabinet that may be one of first kitchen cabinets built by the Hoosier Manufacturing Company.

Oak kitchen cabinet. Circa 1900. The bin in the center of the upper section was probably used for sugar. The deep bin on the right side of the base unit could have been used to hold a large sack of flour. A few months after photographing this cabinet, I ran across a 1900 advertisement by the Hoosier Manufacturing Company showing a cabinet almost identical to the one shown here. After studying the two cabinets, I am reasonably certain this is one the first kitchen cabinets made by Hoosier.

Oak kitchen cabinet. Circa 1900. This turn-of-the-century cabinet with glass paneled doors is now used as a china cabinet. The bin-type drawers at the bottom of the cabinet could have been used for flour or other bulk staples. Manufacturer is unknown.

Five-legged kitchen cabinet. Circa 1905. This cabinet get its name from the pull-out work top that is supported by a single leg in the center. These cabinets were popular just after the turn of the century. This large oak cabinet includes a dry sink. The upper section has two long doors and one short door with full glass panels. The four drawers below the short door were probably used for tableware and kitchen utensils. The pull-out bin on the right side of the base section was mounted on casters so that it could support a large sack of flour. The manufacturer is unknown.

Oak kitchen cabinet. Circa 1910. This cabinet has etched glass panels in the upper doors and a wood work top. Two small swing down bins are included in the upper section. This cabinet is believed to have been built by Wilson of Grand Rapids, Michigan.

Oak kitchen cabinet. Circa 1915. This rare old cabinet has a marble work top. The upper doors have slag glass panels. There was probably a small flour bin mounted in the upper left compartment. Manufacturer is unknown.

Oak kitchen cabinet. Circa 1916. This large cabinet is solid oak and very heavy. The flour bin is behind the long door on the left. The drawer just below the door has a metal lining and was used to catch the flour dispensed from the sifter. There is a narrow roll door just below the center door with the etched glass panel. The cabinet is painted green over its original natural oak finish. This photograph was taken just before the cabinet was sent out to be stripped and restored to its original finish. The manufacturer is unknown.

Wilson kitchen cabinet. Circa 1917. This oak cabinet included a large flour bin, a swing out sugar jar, and opalescent glass panels at the top of the upper doors. The porcelain work top is about an inch wider than the base on each side. This required extra deep side brackets as shown on the right side of the above cabinet.

Greencastle cabinet. Circa 1917. This oak cabinet was built by the Greencastle Cabinet Company of Greencastle, Indiana. The upper doors include opalescent slag glass panels. The two vertical roll doors are similar to the Hoosier roll doors.

Ideal kitchen cabinet. Circa 1920. This oak cabinet was made by the Ideal Cabinet Company of Evansville, Indiana. It has etched glass panels in the upper doors. The long door on the left hid a large flour bin. A roll up tambour door is located beneath the two upper doors on the right. Note that the porcelain work top is somewhat wider than the cabinet.

Wilson cabinet. Circa 1920. This cabinet features etched glass panels in the upper doors and an aluminum covered work top. The flour bin is located on the back of the upper left door which pulls out for filling. The sugar jar is mounted on a bracket that allows it to swing out for filling. A rolling pin rests on supports just below the spice rack. The wire racks on the lower doors were probably used for salt, baking powder, and other staples.

Child's kitchen cabinet. Circa 1925. Some kitchen cabinet manufacturers built scaled-down cabinets for children. These cabinets were usually offered during Christmas sales promotions. The above cabinet is displayed at the Henry County Historical Society in New Castle, Indiana. This cabinet is believed to have been made by The Hoosier Manufacturing Company.

Plainview kitchen cabinet. Circa 1927. This cabinet was manufactured by McDougall for Montgomery Ward who sold it under the Plainview name. The white enameled cabinet is very similar to McDougall cabinets made at that time. Montgomery Ward cabinets were made by Sellers until about 1925.

8

Restoring Hoosier Cabinets

For many years people have been discovering the rewards of restoring and refinishing antique furniture. The sturdy oak furniture mass produced in this country in the late 1800s and the early 1900s has become increasingly popular. The interest in "Hoosier" cabinets has grown rapidly in recent years. However, the restoration of these early kitchen cabinets is quite different than restoring other furniture of this era.

The "Hoosier" cabinet is an unique and complex piece of furniture. The manufacturers of these early kitchen cabinets estimated the life of a cabinet to be 10 to 20 years depending on how they were used and maintained. Daily use in the average kitchen would certainly take its toll in wear and tear, especially on hardware and accessories. Most of the "Hoosier" cabinets found today are more than 60 years old. Some of them have been stored in damp basements or leaky barns where they have been subject to water or rodent damage. However, other cabinets are still being found in relatively good condition.

The restoration of a "Hoosier" cabinet can range from cleaning the cabinet and making a few minor repairs to completely rebuilding the cabinet. The time and effort required to restore a cabinet will be determined by the condition of the cabinet. Before any restoration is begun, it is important to determine the overall condition of the cabinet and the steps required to effectively restore it.

Planning Your Restoration Project

Many people have purchased "Hoosier" cabinets with the intention of restoring them "when they get the time." Since these cabinets are usually covered with several coats of old paint, the first thing most people do is start removing the paint. After spending several hours stripping the paint from a couple of doors, they put the cabinet aside until they are motivated again. It is not unusual for the would-be restorer to become discouraged and sell the cabinet. We have bought several cabinets that were partially stripped and then sold because the job was overwhelming. However, with proper planning and knowing how to do the job, restoring a "Hoosier" cabinet can be a rewarding accomplishment.

This old dilapidated cabinet with several coats of paint might discourage some restorers. However, it did not discourage Miss Terry Upperman of Anderson, Indiana who restored the cabinet as a 4-H project.

The finished cabinet is shown on display at the 1988 Indiana State Fair. Hard work and determination paid off for Miss Upperman. Not only did she win a blue ribbon, she is now the proud owner of a beautiful and unique cabinet.

You should begin your restoration project by carefully examining the cabinet to determine just what needs to be done. Check the cabinet for missing or broken hardware. Make sure that the drawers, doors, and other major components are complete. Check the panels for water damage. Make a list of missing parts and note obvious repairs that will be required. If the cabinet has several coats of paint, some damage may not be apparent until the cabinet has been stripped.

This 1923 Hoosier cabinet will be used for many of the examples shown in this section. The cabinet had been stripped by a previous owner but never finished. There is water damage to three of the doors, the back, and two of the upper side panels. The fabric backing on the roll doors has stretched causing the doors to bind.

Stripping the Cabinet

In most cases, it will be necessary to refinish the cabinet. This means that the old finish will have to be removed. If you are fortunate, the cabinet will still have its original finish which should be fairly easy to remove. However, many cabinets found today are coated with several layers of paint. If this is the case, you may want to consider sending the cabinet out to a professional stripper.

Your cabinet should be completely disassembled before it is stripped. This means removing all of the drawers, doors, racks, and other parts of the cabinet. The flour bin and other accessories should also be removed from the cabinet. The flour bins can usually be easily removed from most cabinets. However, the flour bins used in most Hoosier Manufacturing Co. cabinets are permanently mounted in the cabinet. Removing the flour bin from a Hoosier cabinet is not an easy job but it should be removed to properly strip the cabinet. If you have decided that removing the flour bin is too much of a job, at least remove the sifter head.

The Hoosier cabinet has been completely disassembled for stripping and sanding. Since the cabinet will require only a light stripping to remove the tung oil finish applied by the previous owner, it was not necessary to remove the flour bin. The wood is rather rough and the cabinet will require a thorough sanding. Note the two side panels that have been replaced on the right side of the upper section.

The first step in removing a Hoosier flour bin is to remove the back from the upper section of the cabinet. After the cabinet back has been removed, you will see a wood frame behind the flour bin. This frame is nailed to the cabinet and to the flour bin. Before removing the frame it is a good idea to make a sketch of it so that it can be easily reassembled. The flour bin is nailed to the frame and to the cabinet from the inside. After the frame has been removed, the nails holding the flour bin to the cabinet must be removed from inside the bin. The flour bin can easily be taken out of the cabinet after all of the nails have been removed. If the flour bin has also been painted, it will be much easier to strip after it has been removed from the cabinet.

The Hoosier flour bin is shown with the back removed from the cabinet. The frame behind the flour bin and the nails inside the bin must be removed before the flour bin can be taken out of the cabinet. The sugar bin shown on the left is easily removed.

The hardware should be carefully removed before the cabinet is stripped. If the original hardware will be used, store the hinges and latches in marked plastic bags so that they can be reinstalled on the same doors they were removed from. If the cabinet has several coats of paint, it will probably be necessary to remove the paint from the screws slots so that the screws can be removed without damaging them.

The cabinet will be much easier to strip and refinish if the back panels are removed from the base unit and the upper section. Since the back panels are often warped and damaged, it is usually necessary to replace them. This will be covered later in this section.

Once the cabinet has been disassembled it is ready to be stripped. There are several good strippers available on the market today. We happen to like *Kutzit*, a liquid stripper made by The Savogran Co. However, other refinishers have their own preferences when it comes to strippers. Whatever stripper is used, it should be remembered that these chemicals are rather dangerous and the proper precautions should be exercised when using them. Stripping gloves should be worn to protect the skin and goggles are recommended for eye protection. The stripping should be done in a well-ventilated area. Follow the manufacturer's instructions precisely.

If you decide to send your cabinet out to a professional furniture stripper, you should know what kind of process will be used. Many commercial strippers still use hot or cold dip tanks where the furniture is completely immersed in the stripping solution. This process often causes glued joints to come loose and has a tendency to raise the grain of the wood. Hand stripping is the preferred method, but many commercial strippers do not hand strip because it is time consuming and costly. An alternative process is the Flow-Over method where the piece to be stripped is placed in a large trough and the stripping solution is allowed to flow over the furniture until the finish is removed.

Repairs

After the cabinet has been stripped any necessary repairs should be made before the cabinet is refinished. All loose joints should be reglued. Broken or missing wood components should be repaired or replaced. We stock roll doors or tambours to fit most cabinets. Paneled doors can be made to order. Drawer fronts and other wood parts can usually be made by local craftsmen.

Do not wait until the cabinet has been refinished before deciding what hardware you will use. If the original hardware is all there and is in reasonably good condition, use the original hardware. If some of the hardware is missing, determine if replacements are available for the missing hardware. If not, it may be necessary to replace all the hardware so the it will match. In this case, it may be necessary to fill in the old holes that will not be covered by the new hardware. This should be done before the cabinet is refinished. Now is the time to decide what hardware to use for your cabinet. If you plan to use new hardware, buy it now and make sure that it will work before going ahead with your restoration project. Hardware will be discussed in more detail later in this section.

If the back panels are warped or damaged, they should be replaced. An ideal replacement for these panels is 1/4" luan plywood which is very similar to the plywood originally used by most cabinet manufacturers. A four foot by eight foot sheet of 1/4" luan plywood can usually be obtained from building supply stores for less than $10. Pine or fir plywood is not recommended because of the coarse grain. Birch plywood can also be used but it is usually somewhat more expensive than luan.

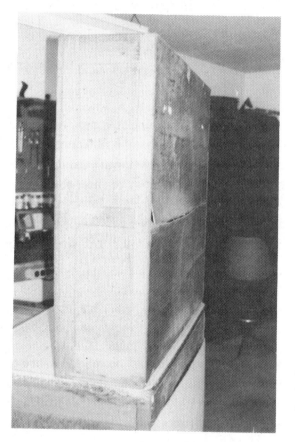

The back panels on the upper section are warped and water-damaged. Although the original back on the upper section consisted of two pieces, it will be replaced by a single panel. The back panel on the base unit had been replaced by a piece of fiber board. Note that the side brackets that hold the upper section to the base unit are missing.

A common problem is warped or water-damaged door and side panels. If the cabinet is oak, these panels are usually oak plywood. Although 1/4" oak plywood is readily available, these panels are often slightly less than 1/4" thick. The door frame or cabinet frame must be taken apart to replace these panels. Unless you are an experienced woodworker this is usually a job for the professional.

This side panel is warped and split due to water damage. The panel above is also damaged. Both panels will be replaced.

New back panels have been cut from 1/4" luan plywood. The inside of the back panels will be stained and finished before they are nailed to the cabinet. The upper section and base unit of the cabinet are shown in the background.

A new back panel is being nailed to the upper section of the cabinet. The interior side of the back panel has been stained and finished.

Refinishing the Cabinet

After the cabinet has been stripped and any necessary repairs have been made, you are ready to refinish it. The first step is to thoroughly sand the cabinet. Although hand sanding is preferable, a power sander can be used for panels and other large flat areas. The best type of sander to use is a palm-held finishing sander. NEVER use a rotary sander.

All of the sanding dust and residue should be wiped from the cabinet before it is stained. The choice of a stain and its application is important. The type of wood is a major factor in choosing a stain. If the cabinet is oak, we prefer a golden oak stain. Cabinets that were originally painted are usually made from gumwood, poplar, or other less desirable woods. Many painted cabinets were made from mixed woods. A darker stain such as walnut will probably look better on these cabinets. Some people apply the stain with a brush and then wipe it off to achieve the desired color. Others simply apply the stain with a rag and then wipe it off.

After the cabinet has been stained and allowed to dry thoroughly, you are ready to apply the finish coats. Although there are several types of finish, we prefer polyurethane varnish for "Hoosier" cabinets. Polyurethane is a durable finish and resists most stains. We normally apply three coats of polyurethane, sanding the cabinets with fine sandpaper between each coat. The sanding residue must be thoroughly removed from the cabinet before the next coat is applied. After the final coat is applied, the finish should be rubbed down with #0000 steel wool.

Some refinishers prefer a lacquer finish because it dries quickly and provides a relatively durable finish. Others simply apply a good wood wax or even tung oil to the stained cabinet. However, in our opinion, neither of these finishes provide the durability of polyurethane or lacquer.

The new back panels are stained with walnut stain. Two coats are used to make the back panels darker than the rest of the cabinet.

This view of the finished cabinet shows the side panels that have been replaced and the new back panels. New side brackets have also been installed.

This is the finished Hoosier cabinet. It is now used as a desk in our shipping room.

Roll Doors

The roll doors or tambours are usually held together by cloth strips glued to the wood slats. After so many years these cloth strips dry out, rot, stretch, or break. As a result the roll door will not open and close properly or it may just fall apart. If you are stripping the cabinet, it will also be necessary to strip the roll door. In order to strip and sand the wood slats, the roll door must be taken apart. Before removing the fabric strips holding the roll together, number each slat on the back so that the door can be reassembled with the slats in the original order.

When refinishing the door, the backs of the slats can be stained but they should not be varnished. After the slats have been refinished, the door can be reassembled by constructing a simple jig consisting of two wood strips placed at a right angle to each other. The strips can be nailed to a workbench top or to a piece of 3/4" plywood large enough to accommodate the roll. Use a square to make sure that the slats are at a right angle.

Place the slats face down in the jig in the same order that they were originally assembled. Make sure that the slats are evenly aligned in the jig. The fabric strips are replaced by a single-piece fabric backing. We use a light weight canvas material called *drill* which can be purchased at most fabric stores. If you are rebuilding a horizontal roll such as a Sellers, the backing should be cut so that its height is the same as the roll. The width of the backing should be trimmed so that about three inches of the slats are exposed on each end.

If the roll is a vertical roll such as used by the Hoosier Manufacturing Company, the width of the backing should be the same as the width of the roll. The height of the backing should be trimmed so that about three inches of the slats are exposed at the top and bottom of the roll. After the backing has been cut, lay it out on the roll door to make sure that it has been cut to the proper size.

Next, mix white wood glue with water until it has about the same consistency as thick paint. Use a paint brush to evenly coat one side of the backing with the glue mixture. Apply the glue in a thin, even coat. Carefully position the glued backing on the roll door and smooth it out with your hands. Make sure that the slats are even and close together and that they remain properly aligned in the jig.

After the backing has been glued down, place a piece of plywood on the backing and weight it down until the glue sets. After about 30 minutes remove the weighted plywood and check the roll door to make sure that the slats are even and straight and not glued together. Let the glue completely dry (two or three hours) before installing the roll door.

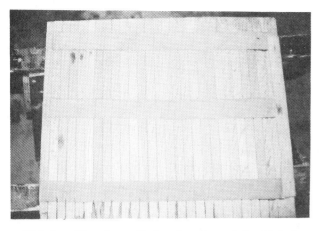

This is a Hoosier roll showing the original fabric strips that hold the roll together.

The wood slats are stripped individually after the old fabric strips have been removed.

After the wood slats have been refinished, they are placed in a jig to keep them straight and aligned. The slats are numbered so that they can be reassembled in the original order.

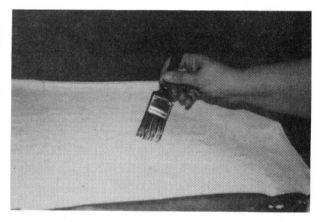

After the new backing is cut to size, one side is coated with a mixture of white wood glue and water.

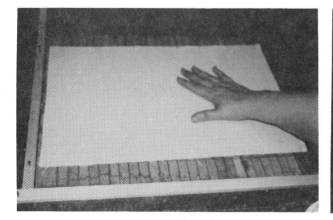

The new fabric backing is pressed down evenly while making sure that the wood slats remain straight and aligned.

The finished roll doors are installed in the cabinet.

Work Tops

If your cabinet was made before 1915, it probably had a metal covered wood work top. Some manufacturers used zinc sheets to cover their wood work tops. However, it was soon discovered that the zinc became toxic when it oxidized and most manufacturers switched to aluminum. The Hoosier Manufacturing Company used aluminum for their work tops as early as 1900. Although Hoosier introduced porcelain work tops about 1915, they continued to offer aluminum covered work tops until 1920.

Since aluminum is relatively soft, it did not hold up well under hard use in the kitchen. Sheet aluminum can be purchased from most metal suppliers. In order to bend and fit the aluminum to the wood work to it is usually necessary to remove the work top. Although the work top will look new after the aluminum has been replaced, it will darken with time.

About 1915 stamped steel work tops with a porcelain enamel finish became popular. The porcelain work tops were easy to clean and were more durable than the aluminum work tops. They were also more sanitary since the hard surface was not easily cut or scratched. However, the porcelain work tops did chip if they were struck hard. If you porcelain work top is chipped, there s not much you can do about it. Although the work top could be refinished, the results are usually less desirable than the chipped top. After all, the cabinet is probably 60 to 70 years old and the chips are part of its character.

If your cabinet had a porcelain work top and it is missing, you may have a problem finding a replacement. At this time no one is making replacement porcelain work tops. Because there are several sizes of porcelain work tops that were used by the various cabinet manufacturers, it would not be practical to manufacture replacements. Occasionally you can find a used porcelain top. We usually have one or two in stock but it may be difficult to find the exact size for a particular cabinet.

Hardware

Hardware is a very important consideration when restoring a "Hoosier" cabinet. Because the hardware was subject to considerable wear and tear, many of the cabinets found today have missing or broken hinges and latches. In some cases the original hardware may have been replaced by modern hardware. If your cabinet has its original hardware and it is in reasonably good condition, by all means use it.

Finding replacement hardware can be a major problem for some cabinets. However, more replacement hardware has become available in the last four or five years. Replacement hardware is now available for most cabinets made by the Hoosier Manufacturing

Company. Because Hoosier made far more cabinets than any other manufacturer and they used the same hardware for many years, there is much more demand for Hoosier hardware.

HOOSIER HARDWARE The hardware shown here was used by the Hoosier Manufacturing Company. The oval latch shown in the upper left was used from about 1910 to 1922. The embossed "H" latch next to it was used from 1922 to about 1930. The Hoosier hinge shown at the lower left was used from about 1915 to 1931. A larger version of the same hinge was used for the larger door on the cabinet base. The drawer knob with the screw in the center was used by Hoosier from at least 1905 to about 1931. Replacements are available for all the Hoosier hardware shown above.

Although Sellers was the second largest manufacturer of early kitchen cabinets, there is very little exact replacement hardware available for Sellers cabinets. Because Sellers changed their hardware often, there is not sufficient demand for most Sellers hardware to justify reproducing it. McDougall used the same hardware for several years but there are no replacements for McDougall hardware at this time. With the exception of the latch that held the Auto-Front door closed, the McDougall hardware was probably the most durable hardware used on "Hoosier" style cabinets. Most McDougall hardware found today is still in relatively good condition.

SELLERS HARDWARE Some of the hardware used by G.I. Sellers & Sons is shown above. Sellers used several styles of hinges and latches on their cabinets. The hinge and latch shown at the top were used on many Sellers cabinets made from the early 1920s to about 1927. The glass knob shown on the left was standard for most Sellers cabinets from about 1915 to the early 1930s. The latch on the lower right was used in the late 1920s. Replacements are available for the Sellers "S" latch, the glass knob and three styles of Sellers hinges.

If you are able to use the original hardware, it may be necessary to remove paint or rust from the hardware. Paint can be removed from hardware by immersing it in paint remover for a few minutes and then removing the paint with a wire or nylon stripping brush. After removing the paint, we use a medium wire wheel brush mounted on a bench grinder to clean the hardware. The wire wheel brush can also be used to remove rust from old hardware. This method can also be used to clean the mounting screws for the hardware. Care must be exercised when using a powered wire wheel brush. We recommend using vise-grip pliers to hold the hardware and protect you hands and wearing goggles for eye protection. If the hardware is nickel-plated, the wire wheel brush will probably remove any remaining nickel plate. Although you can usually have the hardware replated, custom plating is relatively expensive.

One of the most important hardware items for "Hoosier" cabinets are the metal side brackets that hold the top section of the cabinet to the base unit. These brackets are also called "slides" since they allow the work top to be pushed back or pulled out as needed. Until recently, replacement side brackets were almost impossible to find. Cabinets with missing side brackets were often sold cheap because of the difficulty of obtaining replacement brackets. Side brackets are now available to fit most cabinets and they are relatively inexpensive. We currently stock four styles of side brackets including exact replacements for many cabinets.

Sellers side bracket. A similar replacement is available.

Hoosier side bracket. The bracket shown here is a new replacement side bracket.

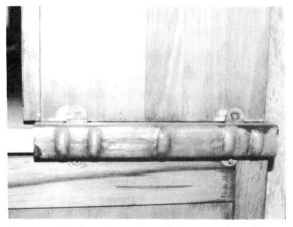

Boone side bracket. A replacement bracket is available.

Side bracket used by Wilson and other cabinet manufacturers. An exact replacement is available.

If your cabinet has missing or broken hardware and exact replacements are not available, there are two or three options to consider. The ideal solution is to replace the broken or missing hardware with the same hardware from another cabinet. However, finding used hardware is becoming very difficult if not impossible. If one or two pieces need replacement, it may be possible to use hardware from the base unit and then replace the hardware on the base unit where it will be less noticeable. Finally, if you cannot find hardware to match the original hardware, you can replace all of the hardware. In some cases this is the only practical solution.

NAPANEE HARDWARE The hardware shown above was used by Coppes Brothers for their Napanee Dutch Kitchenet cabinets. The latch shown in the upper left, the hinge, and the bin pull were used from about 1914 to the early 1920s. Other hinge styles were also used on the Napanee Dutch Kitchenet cabinets. The latch shown on the right was used from about 1922 to the early 1930s. Replacements are available for the hinge and the bin pull. A replacement latch similar to the latch shown on the right is available.

Most of the original hardware used on "Hoosier" style cabinets was nickel-plated steel. Although this hardware was bright and shiny when new, most of it has turned dark with age. In some cases, the nickel plating has worn off and the hardware is rusted. Much of the replacement hardware is available today in either brass or nickel-plated brass. Unless the original hardware is in very good condition, adding shiny nickel-plated replacement hardware will be quite obvious. We suggest using brass hardware and darkening it with *Brass Ager*, an aging solution we sell that makes new brass hardware look old. Simply place the new hardware in the aging solution a watch it until it has reached the desired color. Remove the hardware from the solution, rinse it with clear water, and dry it with a clean cloth. Of course if your old hardware is still bright nickel-plated, you will probably want to use nickel-plated replacement hardware.

MCDOUGALL HARDWARE The McDougall latch and hinge shown above were used from about 1912 to the late 1920s. The cast handle shown here replaced the stamped drawer pulls that were used by McDougall until about 1920. The latch shown on the right was used to hold the McDougall Auto-Front roll door in the closed position. Replacement hardware available for the McDougall cabinets include two styles of hinges and the latch for the Auto-Front roll door.

Often it is more practical to replace all of the original hardware, especially if it is bad condition. We prefer using brass hardware and aging it so that it looks old. In our opinion, installing bright new hardware on an old kitchen cabinet or any other antique looks gaudy and out of place. Some people still like the new brightly polished hardware. Its just a matter of personal preference. If you are restoring cabinets for resale, we recommend that you use aged brass hardware to obtain a more authentic look.

BOONE HARDWARE Some of the hardware used by Campbell-Smith-Ritchie Company for their Boone cabinets is shown above. The latch at the upper left was used on Boone cabinets from about 1912 to the early 1920s. The latch on the right, the hinge, and the drawer pull were used for most Boone cabinets built in the 1920s. Exact replacements are available for the latch shown on the right, the hinge and the drawer pull. The hinge shown above was also used by Sellers and other cabinet manufacturers. It is the most popular replacement hinge we sell.

Although there are several photographs of "Hoosier" style cabinets in this book, most of them do not show the hardware in detail. In this section we have included close-up photographs of the hardware used on Hoosier, Sellers, Napanee, McDougall and Boone cabinets. The captions with these photographs identify the cabinet manufacturer and provide information about replacement hardware.

Some of the replacements hinges we stock for old kitchen cabinets are shown above. The hinge at the upper left is our most popular replacement hinge. It was used by Boone, Sellers, and other cabinet manufacturers. The hinge below it has a slightly different shape and was also used by many cabinet manufacturers. The two hinges shown in the center are replacements for the hinges used by the Hoosier Manufacturing Company. The hinges on the right were used by Napanee and other manufacturers.

Flour Bins and Other Accessories

One of the most distinguishing features of "Hoosier" cabinets is the metal flour bin. The early kitchen cabinet had wood flour bins in the base unit. Some of these bins were mounted on casters and held full sacks of flour. The Hoosier Manufacturing Company introduced the flour bin with a sifter about 1900.

The McCormick & Sons Hardware in Albany, Indiana had a tin shop in the back room where they fabricated custom orders for sheet metal products. The Hoosier Manufacturing Company, which was also located in Albany at that time, placed their first order for 25 sugar bins with McCormick in April of 1900. In addition to the sugar bins, McCormick also made the hopper and sifter bowl for the Hoosier flour bin. As shown on page 23, the body of the first Hoosier flour bins was wood and the hopper and sifter bowl were metal.

McCormick & Sons soon began receiving orders from other cabinet manufacturers for flour bins, sugar bins, bread boxes, and metal table tops. Eventually most major cabinet manufacturers were using McCormick flour bins and other accessories including side brackets. In 1907 Robert B. McCormick, the founder, retired and sold the business to his three sons and the company name then was changed to McCormick Brothers.

By 1910 the Hoosier Manufacturing Company had become so large that they began making their own flour bins. However, McCormick continued to supply most other cabinet manufacturers including G.I. Sellers & Sons. McCormick Brothers sold the hardware store in 1910 to concentrate on their metal fabricating business. The company continued to expand its product line adding such items as hand-held flour sifters and wire shelves for refrigerators. About 1972 McCormick sold most of their tinware business to another Indiana company who continued to manufacturer flour bins, bread boxes, and other items related to the kitchen cabinet industry.

The production of flour bins was discontinued late in 1986, primarily because the product was so labor intensive. More than 50 hand operations are required to make a flour bin. We sold our last flour bins in 1987 and have been unable find anyone else to make them. Hopefully, flour bins will be available again in the future.

Some other cabinet accessories that are available include the swing-out sugar jars, roll doors, wire door racks, door charts and the carousel and spice jars used by Hoosier. Name labels are available for Hoosier, Sellers, Boone, McDougall, and Wilson. Some of the original coffee jars, tea jars, and spice are also available. A few years ago it was common to buy junk cabinets just for the parts. However, junk cabinets with usable parts are very difficult to find.

Flour Bins Available Again

Shortly after the first printing of this book, we were able to purchase many of the original McCormick dies, fixtures, and machines used to manufacture flour bins. Although it took several months to locate additional equipment and materials, we began producing the flour bins again in 1990. We are currently manufacturing eight different flour bins including a replacement for the Hoosier built-in flour bin. We also have a replacement sifter bowl for both McCormick and Hoosier flour bins.